Sketches of Yesterday and Today in Nevada County

By the Same Author
Published by the Nevada County Historical Society:

Nuggets of Nevada County History

*A Tale of Two Cities and a Train: History of the
Nevada County Narrow Gauge Railroad, 1874–1942*

Sketches of Yesterday and Today in Nevada County

by Marilyn Starkey
and Juanita Kennedy Browne

Nevada County Historical Society
Nevada City, California

© *Copyright 1988 by Marilyn Starkey and Juanita Kennedy Browne*
Published by the Nevada County Historical Society
P. O. Box 1300, Nevada City, CA 95959
Designed and produced by Dave Comstock

Library of Congress Cataloging-in-Publication Data

Starkey, Marilyn.
    Sketches of yesterday and today in Nevada County / by
Marilyn Starkey and Juanita Kennedy Browne.
      p.   cm.
    Bibliography: p.
    Includes index.
    ISBN 0-915641-02-X
    1. Nevada County (Calif.)—History, 2. Nevada County (Calif.)
in art. 3. Historic buildings—California—Nevada County. I.
Browne, Juanita Kennedy. II. Title.
F868.N5S66 1988
979.4'37—dc19   88-22584
                                                CIP

*This book is dedicated to the
Indians and the Chinese,
who deserved a better deal.*

About the Artist

MARILYN STARKEY lives in a rustic log home near Nevada City with her husband, Bob, children, Eric and Mia, four cats, one golden retriever, and a lively green parrot.

After graduating from the University of Southern California with a degree in Elementary Education, Marilyn traveled to Europe and moved to Hermosa Beach to teach kindergarten. She returned to school to study painting and ceramics, traveled in the Greek Islands and the Hawaiian Islands, sold her art work at Berkeley's Arts Co-op and the Oakland Museum Store, became a fourth grade teacher's aide and, most recently, studied real estate. She and her husband own and operate Nevada City Real Estate in the historic New York Hotel. Among her favorite books is *How to Raise Children at Home in Your Spare Time*.

In 1983 Marilyn won "Best Nevada County Scene" and first place in mixed media at the Nevada County Fair. Her art work was chosen for the catalog cover for the 1987 Sierra Visuals show. She says she gets her artistic abilities from her mother, Mabel Austin, a talented painter who lives in nearby Penn Valley.

About the Author

JUANITA KENNEDY BROWNE was born in Oklahoma and moved to California with her parents shortly after World War II. She worked as a technical editor for Douglas Aircraft in Long Beach and later for Aerojet-General in Sacramento. In 1962 she had a career change. While raising a second family, she continued her education, received a Master of Arts degree in English with a history minor from California State University, Sacramento, and began freelance writing. Hundreds of her articles have been published in local, regional, and national newspapers and magazines.

In 1973 Juanita and her husband, Pete, and their two youngest sons, Juan and Dana, moved to their Christmas tree ranch in The Hollow near Grass Valley.

Since 1979 Juanita has written a monthly column for the Grass Valley *Union* on events 100 years ago in Nevada County. Her first book, *Nuggets of Nevada County History*, was published by the Nevada County Historical Society in 1983 and is now in its third printing. In 1987 the Society published her second book, *A Tale of Two Cities and a Train: History of the Nevada County Narrow Gauge Railroad, 1874–1942*.

For her contributions in the interpretation and preservation of Nevada County history through her books, articles, and presentations, Juanita received an award from the Nevada County Historical Society in 1985, a Certificate of Commendation from The American Association for State and Local History in 1986, and Awards of Merit from the California Historical Society and the Conference of California Historical Societies in 1988.

Contents

List of Sketches

Introduction

Sketch: 1. A drawing representing the chief features of an object or scene. 2. A short literary composition intentionally slight in treatment, discursive in style, and familiar in tone.
Sketchbook: A book of or for sketches.
—Webster's New Collegiate Dictionary

THIS BOOK IS A SKETCHBOOK that features mixed media sketches of well-known and lesser-known scenes in Nevada County fleshed out by simple word sketches that tell a few familiar and unfamiliar facts and incidents related to those scenes.

Historians often shoehorn in all the quibbling details of their subject. Sketchers don't. This sketchbook is not intended to exhaust either the subject or the reader. I disagree with a few of the details on some of the historic plaques that mark some of these scenes, and some of the plaques disagree with each other. However, I don't feel a sketchbook is the place to air possible historical errors. Besides, a few years here or there shouldn't detract from the overall historic significance of a spot, and I'm sure a slight mistake in a date will not cause the general reader many sleepless nights. Still, I have tried to keep the historical data as concise and correct as possible.

What was here yesterday is not here today, and yet it is. What is here today may well be gone tomorrow, and yet it stays. These sketches are an attempt to capture the ephemeral nature of a living, vibrant, changing, growing community and blend yesterday with today and preserve the essence for tomorrow.

Historic Spots in Nevada City

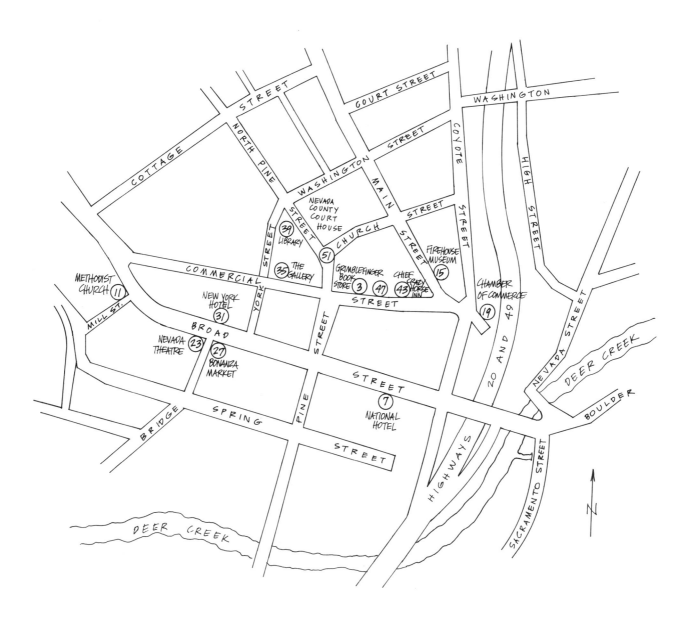

Note: Circled numbers identify pages on which sketches of these historic sites appear.

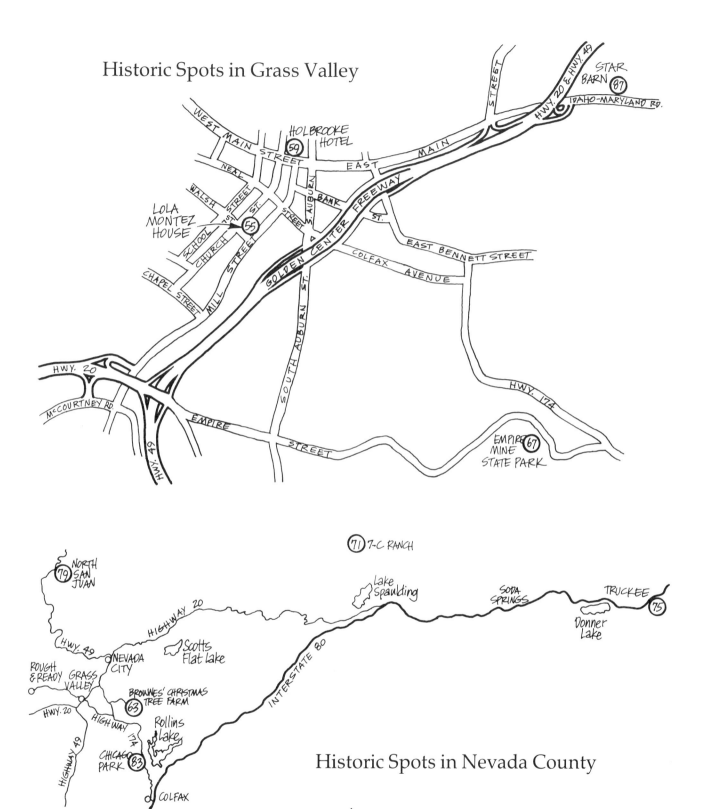

Historic Spots in Grass Valley

Historic Spots in Nevada County

It Was Written

It Was Written

IN THE BEGINNING there was the word: "Gold!" The word that appeared in letters, newspapers, and reports and told of the fabulous riches to be picked up in fabled California. The word that brought wealth to a few, but lured many others to suffering, hardship, and death. The word that led to an outpouring of letters and newspaper items that led, in turn, to guidebooks, advertisements, songs, and cartoons in which could be found both snippets of hard reality and doses of dangerous fiction.

The slow leakage of the news of the gold discovery in Coloma in January 1848 was generally ignored as a sham until Sam Brannan checked out the story and found it to be true. Shrewd Sam, who foresaw the vast profits to be made by selling supplies and equipment to eager prospectors, bought all the gold mining supplies he could find and pulled one of the first California-style publicity stunts. In May 1848, he ran wild-eyed with faked excitement through the muddy streets of San Francisco waving a bottle filled with gold and shouting "Gold! Gold! Gold from the American River!" That did it. The word was out, and the rush was on.

The word was soon heard in parlors, pubs, and pulpits throughout the world. Newspapers eagerly printed anything they could find on the subject from official reports to private letters and journals written by earlier explorers, adventurers, soldiers, and emigrants. Thousands were smitten by those words and were eager to join the rush to rich but remote and mythical California. The big questions were: How do I get there from here? Where do I find the gold? How do I get it out?

No sooner asked than answered. Book publishers eagerly rushed into print any information they could find on the gold country, old and new, false and true. Paste-and-glue authors churned out guidebooks that claimed to tell all you needed to know about how to get to the gold country, how to get the gold out, and how to get back rich—and soon. One of the first was *The Digger's Handbook* written by D. L. (Damn Liar). Some of these comprehensive guidebooks consisted of less than 30 pages and sold for 25¢ with a map or 12½¢ without a map. The price was right, but it could cost your life. Buying a guidebook without a map was a better buy. Much of the information was not only plagiarized but was dangerously inaccurate. Maps showed routes, water sources, pasture grasses, and mountain passes that did not exist. One recommended sailing 1,000 miles up the Rio Grande, which is not navigable.

One of the most informative early handbooks was a paste-and-glue job by Joseph E. Ware. When Ware set out to follow his own directions, he was stricken by cholera, abandoned by his companions, and died.

Guidebooks weren't the only way to make a quick quarter from words about the gold rush. Songs from the "Gold Digger's Waltz" to the "Sacramento Gallop" were timely hits. When one author ran out of useful information, he filled his pseudo guidebook with songs and poetry as if the emigrant could sing or rhapsodize his way to the golden paradise.

The gold rush also resulted in a creative awakening in advertising. Some suppliers advertised the "bare necessities" in such quantities and varieties that even Hannibal's elephants couldn't have gotten the load across some parts of the trail. Later emigrants just

GRIMBLEFINGER: BOOKS & GALLERY
COMMERCIAL STREET, NEVADA CITY, CALIFORNIA
MARILYN STARKEY

followed the litter of these abandoned necessities.

R. Porter & Co. advertised their Aerial Transportation system as the best route from New York to California. For $50, including board and transportation, you could fly to the gold fields and back in seven days. Operation was to begin on 1 April 1849.

Cartoonists, who came as close to reality as some of the advertisers and guidebooks, had a field day. One cartoon showed a group of passengers astride a long rubber band ready to be beany-flipped into California. With one jerk of the rubber band you could reach your destination.

Thousands of the rushers snapped up these incompetent guidebooks, bought pounds of unnecessary supplies and equipment, and—despite their naivete—made it to California where their hunger for the written word continued to be as insatiable as their hunger for gold. Not only letters from home but newspapers, magazines, and books were in great demand in California. Lonesome 49ers paid up to $8 to have a letter delivered to their remote campsite. In return, they sent thousands of letters home and wrote hundreds of journals. Some were short and dull; others were long and dull. Although not without their triumphs and tragedies, individual experiences were basically unromantic and dull. No matter. Publishers quickly rushed some into print, and readers were generally receptive and uncritical.

Where there's a demand, there's a potential for profit. In the mid-1850s, San Francisco boasted having published more books than the rest of the civilized west. Among the earliest businesses established in Nevada County were bookstores, which, like other stores, did not specialize but diversified. They sold books: school, law, medical, history, poetry, religious, scientific, technical, mining, fraternal, classic, and popular books. They sold local newspapers, fresh off the presses. They sold newspapers from all parts of the world, not-so-fresh off steamer ships in San Francisco. They sold magazines, California and eastern. They sold valentines, Christmas cards, and calling cards; stationery, paper, pens, and ink; musical instruments and sheet music; cutlery, fancy goods, toys, gifts, tobacco, cigars, candy, and sewing machines. On the side, they operated circulating libraries.

As it was in the beginning, so it is now—with a few changes. People are still word-hungry; however, most—not all—bookstores in Nevada County now specialize in selling books, either new or used. Here, at Grimblefinger, you can find the latest best sellers and the classics plus a good selection of books on California and Nevada County—subjects that have lost little of the glitter of their golden past.

For Those Traveling Without a Blanket

For Those Traveling Without a Blanket

As HORDES OF 49ER MINERS first chased the golden rainbow to the streams, rivers, and ravines around present-day Nevada City, placer gold could be found with a little luck and even less experience. With the basic equipment of a pick, shovel, gold pan, strong back, and the endurance of a dumb ox, a few hit it big. However, after prospecting only one hard day some found the pickin's too slim and the workin' too hard and decided to find an easier and drier way to make their pile. It didn't take a lot of smarts to figure out that it was easier to let the younger, hardier miners dig out the gold and then redistribute the wealth by selling them provisions, entertainment, and a few comforts of home at highly inflated prices.

Far and away the most popular and profitable business was running a gaudy combination of saloon, restaurant, gambling hall, and hurdy-gurdy house, which was *not* a musical instrument. Next, came operating a hotel or boarding house that also offered food, comfort, and shelter—of sorts.

One of the first boarding houses in Nevada City was opened in March 1850 by a lucky miner who had a hard-working wife, Madame Penn. In April 1850, the Nevada Hotel, a 38- x 48-foot wooden structure made from one tree, was filled with 40 boarders who paid $25 a week.

These early hovels were hotels in name only, and such names they had, from the simple to the grand. By 1851, Nevada City boasted the Placer, Pioneer, American, Bryce, and Nevada Hotels and the Virginia, Washington, Nevada City, and Missouri Houses. At the Hotel de France "all persons traveling without a blanket" could board for $14 a week or only $11 if you were so busy mining you ate only two meals a day.

As it was in all early mining camps, the Fire King repeatedly changed the face of the camps—usually for the better. After Nevada City was wiped out by fire on 11 March 1851, a newspaper correspondent declared the commodious stores, saloons, and hotels that were rapidly going up would give the town a far better appearance than it formerly had. Typically, Barker's Exchange, a saloon, was "by far the best building in town." In size, taste, elegance, and beauty it surpassed many—if not all—such buildings in Sacramento and San Francisco.

Nevada City was here to stay even if Barker's Exchange and most of the newly rebuilt stores and hotels were not. Then, in 1856 came the National Exchange, now the National Hotel, which on a historic plaque on the front of the building is hailed as one of the oldest hotels in continuous operation west of the Rockies and also the "site of the first whipping post in California."

On this site in April 1851, a lynch judge and jury after two days of deliberation sentenced three men to 39 lashes each for stealing $2,600 in gold dust. Contrary to the facts on the plaque, the lashes were "laid on" on a hill southeast of town; however, the brutal punishment got results. It "discouraged" thefts for several months.

The Fire King struck Nevada City again and again, and each time the city was rebuilt on the cooling ashes. Each time the National was damaged or demolished by fire, it was also rebuilt.

By 1859, stagecoaches porcupined with pas-

1854
THE NATIONAL HOTEL AT CHRISTMAS
NEVADA CITY, CALIFORNIA
MARILYN STARKEY

sengers, mail, and express material came and went in all directions from the National. The "thoroughly fireproof" three-story hotel advertised new beds and furniture and several apartments fitted up in a style that could not be surpassed. Tables were supplied with the best the markets offered, game suppers were "got up to order," and the bar was open all night.

In 1888, Dexter Ridley, a night clerk at the hotel, claimed that for 27 years, except when he was out of town temporarily, he ate every meal at the same table in the same chair in the National Hotel dining room.

In 1895, President-to-be Herbert Hoover checked in at the National Hotel, a favorite hangout for mining men. Since he was a young and nearly broke Stanford University mining graduate looking for a job, proprietors John and Bayliss Rector extended him a line of credit until he got a menial job pushing ore cars in the Reward Mine.

Here, in 1902 the world-famous coloratura soprano, Emma Nevada, born in nearby Alpha Diggin's, stepped onto the balcony to bow and wave to her wildly cheering fans before her concert in the Nevada Theatre. That balcony is still the favorite spot for dignitaries to watch the annual Constitution Day parade, Father's Day bicycle race, the alternate-year Fourth of July parade, and any other parade that passes that way—and all of them do.

Sunday Services—A Fall from Grace

Sunday Services—A Fall from Grace

ALTHOUGH MALE SOCIETY in the rough and tough California mining camps had little resemblance to the genteel female-centered society the 49ers had left behind, Sunday was still a day set aside for the miners to renew their spirits, take stock, and clean up their act. On Sunday they washed their extra shirt, then trekked into town to lay in a stock of supplies and renew their spirits in a gambling saloon. Few sought out either preachers or churches as there were few or none. However, pastors soon sought out their far-astray flocks.

Itinerant preachers would hold services wherever they could find a crowd that would listen. Since the largest crowds were usually gathered in the saloons, that's where the preachers preached. The gambling would stop while the minister led the boys in singing a few hymns, said a few words, and took up a collection. The miners were usually attentive and generous; however, as soon as the minister went out the door, the drinking and gambling went on.

Services were also held in rude cabins and under spreading shade trees, and denominations made little difference. On a typical Sunday in Nevada City in 1850, the hymn of a small congregation soared heavenward accompanied by the bellows of a mule auctioneer, a drunken rendition of "Auld Lang Syne," wheezes of a hand organ, rattles of a tambourine, shouts of packers unloading supplies, and snarls of a savage dog fight, which drew the largest crowd. Preachers had stiff competition to overcome. Yet, they did overcome, slowly.

The first church in Nevada City, which looked more like a barn than a church, was built on a hillside on Main Street in 1850. The builders didn't even take time to level the ground, and the small, nondenominational congregation had to fight the urge to backslide as they sat on primitive seats tilted on the uneven floor.

Although early congregations were small, pastors and churches began to multiply and divide into distinct denominations, especially when ladies came in to settle, civilize, purify, and raise funds.

To get away from the noise and corruption in the center of town, the Methodist Episcopal Church North built their first church further up Broad Street. However, when would-be worshipers wouldn't hike up the hill, the church was moved to its present location where early pastors had to shout to be heard over the noisy rabble congregated in nearby gambling dens and houses of prostitution.

Ladies were the rocks upon which these early churches were supported. They held donation parties, festivals, fairs, suppers, balls, and benefits to raise money to pay their pastors and to build and rebuild churches that were repeatedly wiped out by King Fire. In February 1855, the flames of a "literal hell" roared for several hours between the Methodist Church South on lower Broad Street and the Methodist Church North on upper Broad. Both churches survived that fire; however, in July 1856, the Methodist Churches, both North and South, and the Catholic and Congregational Churches burned. In 1863, when the fire alarm sounded

FOUNDED
1850
BY ISAAC OWEN

1854

FIRST
METHODIST
CHURCH

MILL
STREET
CINEMA
AND
COFFEE
HOUSE

THE FIRST METHODIST CHURCH
NEVADA CITY, CALIFORNIA
MARILYN STARKEY

during morning services, a minister reminded his hastily departing congregation that services would be held in the evening. By evening, Nevada City and five churches lay in ashes. Only the Baptist Church escaped the holocaust.

Undaunted, the small congregations with the ladies at the forefront raised funds and rebuilt. The ladies also attended church regularly. One preacher took exception with husbands who walked their wives to church and left them at the door while they went in pursuit of a "pandemonium of passions." One Sunday, Adam Bland, who was far from bland, delivered a pointed sermon that pointed so directly toward Mr. Miller's lack of church attendance that Miller confronted the reverend with a mission in mind of giving him a sound thrashing. Although Bland, a most muscular Christian, claimed he only shook Miller "against the ground" during the ensuing discussion, Miller brought charges of assault and battery.

The day of the hearing, the courtroom was crowded with both the holy and the unholy. When all the evidence was in, "Old Zeke," the justice of the peace, decided that Miller started the fight, the fight was fair, Miller got licked, and he deserved it. The fighting parson was acquitted. The holy applauded and the unholy, along with Old Zeke, went for a round of drinks.

A later minister's spunky behavior was greeted not with plaudits but tushes. The more conservative ladies of the Methodist congregation openly clucked disapproval of Mrs. Stump's fancy needlework, and when Parson Stump admitted during a debate that he was fond of dancing, he slipped considerably in their pious esteem. When the pastor took up roller skating, he fell from their grace completely and was forced to seek more liberal pastures. Later, word came back that Stump had abandoned the ministry and was happy and prosperous in his new degradation as a lawyer! The pious were confirmed in their belief; they always knew "that man would go bad entirely!"

As early as 1852, church members requested local merchants to close on Sunday. Some businessmen agreed to do so, and a few actually did; however, not the saloons, never on Sunday.

The pious, however, did not give up the good fight. In 1858, a city ordinance prohibited any amusement after midnight on Saturday. When the clock struck 12 and the musicians played on at a masquerade ball in the Arcade Saloon, the marshal stopped the music and took the musicians into custody. At their hearing, the defendants and their attorney so wore out the subject, the audience, and the justice, they were discharged, and another Sunday ordinance, like many before and after, went unenforced.

The battle goes on with each person marching to the beat of his own beliefs. Nevada City still has more saloons than churches, and they never close on Sundays. Nevada City also has many stately churches with large congregations such as this beautiful historic Methodist Church, which was rebuilt in 1864. Here, worshipers are always welcome.

Hail! To Fire Laddies, Hose Carts, Horses, and History

Hail! To Fire Laddies, Hose Carts, Horses, and History

AFTER PART OF NEVADA CITY WAS wiped out by fire for the second time in September 1852, 38 would-be fire laddies met to organize committees to raise subscriptions to buy equipment for a hook and ladder company that could dampen the Fire King's spirits. They bragged that with 15 strong men and good tools, they could remove a whole block when necessary and stop the Fire King in his tracks. Perhaps they could, but they didn't because they didn't organize.

While the fire laddies fiddled for seven more years and Nevada City burned four more times, city ladies threw a theater benefit and a ball at the courthouse and raised $1,072 for fire fighting equipment. The proceeds were deposited in the bank where they languished.

Local fire fighters didn't lack spunk or spirit. At the cry of "Fire!" merchants and miners joined forces and worked like "heroes on the battlefield" despite scorched clothes, blistered backs, charred faces, injury, and death. Although most agreed that not even a Niagara could have stopped the earlier fires, they simply couldn't agree on whether a hose carriage or a hook and ladder truck would be the most effective weapon against future assaults by the Fire King. Wooden buckets and wet blankets were certainly not doing the job.

Meanwhile, newspapers groused that no other town in California the size of Nevada City was without any means of fire protection—not one fire hose or hydrant or city water system to hook it to.

The Fire King wouldn't wait. In May '60, the almost two-year-old Grass Valley Hook and Ladder Company rushed over to help thwart his most recent attack on Nevada City. Perhaps the flashy showing of the Grass Valley lads flooded the Nevada City lads with admiration. Once the floodwaters were loose, all hesitancy was washed aside. The law allowed one fire company for every 1,000 inhabitants. Nevada City could have three, and three she soon had. The Nevada Hose Company No. 1 organized with 47 members on 12 June 1860. The next day, the Eureka Hose Company No. 2 with 34 members organized. A few days later the Protection Hook and Ladder Company No. 1 organized with 37 members.

By July, Hose Company No. 1's carriage with four wheels and three bells arrived, followed closely by the Eureka Company's magnificent truck purchased from the San Francisco Pennsylvania Hose Company No. 12. In a few weeks the Eureka Company was no more. To save the time and expense of repainting their already beautifully decorated carriage, they simply scratched out the "1" from the "12" and Presto! Eureka became Pennsylvania Hose Company No. 2.

In less than a year, the companies had purchased their basic equipment and snazzy uniforms, had built two permanent brick firehouses, and had access to a good city water supply.

While daring the Fire King to strike again, the fire laddies dashed out to douse chimney and grass fires, drill and parade, polish their equipment and their buttons, promenade at firemen's balls, and clean up the neighborhood by sluicing out a few hurdy-gurdy houses.

In their first big trial by fire in November '63, the companies rushed to the scene, but orders

OLD FIRE HOUSE #1 1861
HOME OF HISTORICAL MUSEUM
MARILYN STARKEY

15

from Chief Engineer Harrington were nowhere to be heard. When last seen he was hustling his "strumpet and her duds" out of a burning hotel. Undaunted, the lads hooked up their hoses, turned on the hydrants, and—nothing. No water pressure. The pipes had become clogged with mud. Once again, Nevada City was destroyed.

Despite these early defeats, the Nevada City Volunteer Fire Department fought fires valiantly and more efficiently year after year. They never completely vanquished the Fire King, but they kept him in check.

The two brick firehouses still stand. At this Main Street firehouse, horses were trained to get into position to be harnessed at the sound of the alarm bell. One horse liked dashing to fires so much, he would open his stall on slow days, give the firebell a yank, get set to be harnessed, and wait for the action to start.

Today, the Nevada County Historical Society's museum in the firehouse of Nevada Hose Company No. 1 is a storehouse of relics that can fire a visitor's imagination with the history preserved inside. Among the treasured exhibits are a splendid collection of Maidu Indian baskets, relics from the Donner Party, priceless Chinese artifacts, and the altar from the How Wong Joss House—one of the oldest in California. The museum also sells books on Nevada County history and historical souvenirs.

Go, Go, Water, Washoe, and Wells, Fargo

Go, Go, Water, Washoe, and Wells, Fargo

THREE INDUSTRIES ESSENTIAL to gold mining were once clustered together where these little buildings now huddle. Moving from left to right were: an extensive and dependable source of water, the South Yuba Canal Mining Company; an experienced and reliable assayer, James J. Ott; a safe and reliable gold transportation service, Wells, Fargo.

Without water, the billions of tons of gold-bearing gravel could never have been washed down from the hillsides; the gold could never have been separated from the gravel; and the debris could never have been washed down streams to inundate and infuriate the flatland farmers below. Without an improved city water system, the town-eating Fire King would have seldom gone hungry, and some of the more conservative citizens would have gone mighty thirsty. Without water, agriculture, viticulture, and horticulture developments would have died on the vine—so to speak. Alas! land developers would have little to boom about, and Nevada County would never have known the electrifying force of hydroelectricity that shot power as far as the San Francisco Bay area.

When the early miners first got the bright idea that it was easier to bring water to their gravel than carry their gravel to water, a serpentine system of water ditches began to snake around the hillsides. In 1854, three rival ditch companies decided they would rather consolidate than fight and formed the tongue-twister Rock Creek, Deer Creek, and South Yuba Canal Company, which became simply the South Yuba Canal Company in 1870. That company, which operated out of this building from 1857 to 1880, went on to build a system of acres of reservoirs and miles and miles of water ditches and flumes. That system, which claimed to be the largest in California, carried water to thousands of miles of connecting water systems that, in turn, carried billions of gallons of water to hundreds of hydraulic mines and eventually became the mammoth Pacific Gas and Electric Company.

Before a miner bought water from one of these mazes of ditches, he needed to know if the dirt he was digging was worth the washing. James J. Ott, who had an assay office next door, could tell you just that, which made some miners rich and saved others their pokes. Ott's assay of a little bag of blue-black dirt in 1859 alerted the world to the richness of the silver deposits just over the hill in Washoe country, which to the consternation of Nevada City and Nevada County usurped their names and became the state of Nevada.

Ott didn't make the first or only survey of Washoe silver, but the results of his assay, which buzzed around by word of mouth and in local newspapers, got miner George Hearst onto his ass and over the mountains to buy two of the richest claims before the owners heard the news. When Hearst returned, he spread

SOUTH YUBA CANAL OFFICE
OTT'S ASSAY OFFICE
NEVADA CITY, CALIFORNIA

19

the word that the claims were really not all that rich, the climate was terrible, and everyone should stay home. Many didn't listen to George, but heeded the cry of "Silver!" and "Go it Washoe!" Some who did, such as Hearst, became millionaires.

Once you had found and refined the gold, you needed a reliable way to transport it for safekeeping or minting. That was the job of Wells, Fargo, which was next door, but is now marked only by a plaque. The original building was conquered by the Freeway King in the 1960s.

Today, the Video Division of the Nevada County Historical Society operates in the left, upper story to capture and preserve the rich history of Nevada County. Below, the Nevada City Chamber of Commerce assays and tells the world about the wealth of that history. Next door on the old Ott's assay site are businesses that come and go, just like Wells, Fargo.

Lynch the Infernal Cuss!

Lynch the Infernal Cuss!

DESPITE THE EARLY primitive paths that took the stamina of a mule to get over, a circus made it to Nevada City as early as 1851, and other entertainment troupes trouped right behind.

Soon after, a local businessman realized how popular these troupers were and slapped an addition onto his two-story grocery-hardware-reading-room building, and Dramatic Hall was born. Boarders who lay stacked like cordwood on tiers of beds in the adjoining hotel could hear the performance through the thin walls—if the histrionics were not drowned out by close-packed snorers.

The entertainment-hungry miners packed such theaters and greeted all kinds of shows with enthusiasm. They were especially receptive to female performers of any age and any degree of talent and would shower them with coins and nuggets. They loved little, once-local Lotta Crabtree, and their golden showers made her wealthy.

Although show business could be profitable for both performers and theater owners, it was a hard business. Even the best performers had to travel great distances over rough territory to reach paying audiences. They sometimes performed on bars and store counters, and miners were as free with their criticism as they were their applause and coins. A terrible actor or a too-convincing villain was sometimes in real danger.

When Hugh F. McDermott murdered his role in *Richard III,* he was pelted with vegetables and garbage and forced to retire from the littered stage when the miners started to shout—with sincerity—"Kill him! Kill him!"

Edwin Booth played Iago with such villainy, miners pulled out their pistols and blazing away at Iago shot off the tip of Othello's nose. Iago-Booth made a hasty exit when the miners started to shout—with feeling—"Lynch the infernal cuss!"

Despite these professional hazards, by 1852 Grass Valley, Rough and Ready, and Nevada City had theaters. However, theaters, like traveling troupes, had a way of coming and going rapidly. In Nevada City, most went up in smoke; but contrary to tradition, the Jenny Lind was carried away by a flood on Deer Creek.

Undaunted by disastrous fires or pathetic performers, another theater would soon go up. Mr. and Mrs. Lyman Frisbie parlayed some of the most lucrative businesses in the area. They operated a theater, a restaurant, and a drinking and ice cream saloon.

When their Nevada Theater (not this one) went up on Main Street in 1856, the local press with their usual home-town hype claimed it compared "favorably" with any theater in the state. The painting on the drop curtain was splendid, the scenery was superb, and the seats were cushioned and comfortable.

Through these early theaters trooped some of the best performers of the time including Edwin Booth, Kate Hayes, Mark Twain, Henry Ward Beecher, Horace Greeley (who took his own advice), Schuyler Colfax (for whom the town was named), Lola Montez (for whom a mine and a hill were named), Emma Nevada (who took the name of the city and state), and James Marshall (who lectured on how he started it all in Coloma).

Gold camp theaters proved to be profitable pickin's not only for owners, actors, singers,

Est. 1865

NEVADA THEATRE

NEVADA
THEATRE
CALIFORNIA'S
OLDEST EXISTING
THEATRE
BUILDING

BRIDGE BROAD

INFORMATION

NEVADA THEATRE
NEVADA CITY, CA
MARILYN STARKEY

23

and dancers but spiritualists, phrenologists, illusionists, tightrope walkers, lecturers, politicians, wrestlers, prizefighters, and circuses. Miners liked their leisure and their theater varied. They patronized Italian opera, French ballet, vulgar farces, intellectual lectures, medicine and minstrel shows, and classical tragedy and comedy. Everything from hesitating Hamlets to bottled elixirs could part the miners from the price of admission, which in 1857 at the first Nevada Theater was $1.50 for dress circle, $1.00 for the parquet, and 50¢ for the pit. Some of the performances were not worth the price of the pits.

When the first Nevada Theater burned, and the Metropolitan Theater was built in 1858, the local press found fault not with the theater per se but the management for sure. J. S. Potter, known as the "Micawber of California," was taken to task for not paying his landlords, his printers, or his actors and for being a bad manager and a worse actor. When the curtain accidentally slipped during a performance, Potter had to stoop even lower than his business behavior to be seen by the audience. Before his stooped soliloquy was finished, the curtain crashed to the delight and relief of the audience. A critic concluded that the whole abominable mess proved that local audiences would pay a dollar to see tragedy turned to farce and comedy butchered.

The Metropolitan Theater burned in 1863 and Nevada City was without staged tragedy or comedy. In late 1864, the Nevada Theatre Association bought the fire-gutted three-story brick Bailey House and sold stock at $100 a share to begin construction of this, the second Nevada Theatre. More than half the stock was sold in one afternoon. Then things slowed down.

After the citizens had gone unentertained by a theatrical company for more than a year, they got restless; so restless they decided to throw a ball to raise enough funds to put the finishing touches on their new theater, which was to be one of the best in the state—or at least this side of San Francisco. The ball held in the theater in June 1865 was a smashing success. At $5 a ticket, more about 300 dancers glided to the strains of the Nevada Quadrille Band under 96 gas lights till daylight with only a break to dine at the Hook and Ladder hall down the street.

On 11 September 1865, this "Magnificent Temple of the Muses" was opened. Here, Mark Twain lectured about his trip to the Sandwich Islands. Here, once-local Cornish tenor Richard Jose and local home-county girl Emma Nevada returned to captivate sellout crowds as they had done throughout the world. Here, local organizations and high school classes staged amateur plays to sellout audiences of doting friends and relatives. In 1908, silent movies and vaudeville acts and, later, "talkies" replaced stage productions. When television lured away audiences, the Nevada Theatre closed in the mid-1950s. In the 1960s, the Liberal Arts Commission formed and through donations and successful fund-raising events bought and restored the theater, which is once again the stage for a diverse array of local and imported talents and productions.

Consciences Cleaned for Fifty Cents

Consciences Cleaned for Fifty Cents

LIFE IN THE MINING CAMPS was a hard life at best. It was a hard life at worst for the Chinese. Everything the Chinese tried to do to eke out a slim living, whites worked to prevent, either legally or illegally.

In 1879, the new California constitution declared that Chinese could not be hired by county municipalities, could not become citizens, and could not inherit or own land. Although the U.S. courts declared these laws and other local anti-Chinese ordinances to be illegal, it didn't stop local communities from enforcing them.

Early ordinances in Nevada City made it illegal for Chinese to live in the city limits or even remain within the limits for more than 24 hours. When the Chinese built their own communities and opened stores and shops to cater to their fellow countrymen, more ordinances were passed to get them moved out.

Since the Chinese were not allowed to own property, whites were urged not to rent to them. The few who did, charged exorbitant prices. If the Chinese built where they weren't wanted, their buildings were simply torn down or burned.

If they were lucky enough to find work in local mines, hotels, or restaurants, those businesses would be boycotted until the Chinese were fired.

When they turned to raising vegetables, Grass Valley levied a license fee on them and a Nevada City ordinance made it illegal for Chinese to carry baskets of produce on city sidewalks.

When they opened laundries, Nevada City charged them a quarterly license fee of $10. When that didn't force them out of business, the quarterly fee was raised to $30.

Even their meager pleasures were outlawed or disrupted. Although the Supreme Court in 1880 ruled that smoking opium was no more illegal than smoking tobacco, Nevada City revoked the Chinese licenses to sell opium. They also outlawed the game of fan tan—a favorite Chinese card game. The "boys" out to have a little "fun" would charge into Chinese brothels, throw out the prostitutes and their clientele, and tear up the joint.

The Chinese were in a "damned if they do and damned if they don't" situation. Local businessmen resented the fact that the Chinese communities imported most of their food and clothing from China and sent their meager savings home. However, if a Chinese tried to buy from a white establishment, prices were jacked sky high, and they were charged excessive fees for white services—if they could get them.

Chinese who wore their traditional dress were ridiculed; yet, when a Chinese gentleman and his lady, dressed in appropriate "western attire," seated themselves in the dress circle of the Nevada Theatre, the boys called the police, and the couple was escorted out to the accompaniment of loud catcalls.

Since Chinese could not testify in court against a white person, they were easy prey and were systematically robbed and sometimes beaten and killed by local thugs. Usually, they gave little resistance; however, when the notorious blackguard, George Washington, a black man, tried to rob a group of Chinese on Deer Creek, they beat him into submission, trussed

BONANZA MARKET
NEVADA CITY, CALIFORNIA
MARILYN STARKEY

him up like a pig on a pole, and carried him off to the law.

Laws were enforced less often and less severely against whites. In 1867 a mob of about 100 drove out the Chinese near French Corral and set fire to their cabins. Of the 27 whites arrested only one was brought to trial. He was found guilty and fined $100. The others were released.

In 1876, members of the Caucasian League set fire to two Chinese cabins on Trout Creek near Truckee and shot and killed one Chinese and wounded another. Although two men confessed to the crime, the first man to be tried was acquitted and six others were never brought to trial.

In contrast, a Chinese was fined $50 for stealing 15 chickens and another was sentenced to 100 days on the chain gang for stealing a slab of bacon. To add insult to injury, "Uncle Billy," the local jailer, cut off their queues.

The Chinese were not without their faults. The kidnapping of Chinese maidens set off several riots among different Chinese factions, and they fought and killed each other for debts as small as 25¢. They had their share of thieves, murderers, and general bad guys; and they did rob sluices and steal chickens and eggs. When Ah Chee was arrested for stealing chicken eggs, he defended himself by declaring they were not chicken eggs but duck eggs. From then on, he was known as "Duck Egg" and was a favorite target—as was any passing Chinese—for boys having a little rock-throwing fun.

As the years passed, the hard old days became the good old days, and the Chinese—most of whom had died or left the county—became somewhat more acceptable when remembered through a patina of nostalgia. In December 1921, a well-known attorney in the bay area had a 40-year-old twinge of conscience over the avalanche of rocks he had thrown at Duck Egg. To ease his conscience and wipe the slate clean for Christmas, he sent Duck Egg a dollar. Suddenly, "old boys" from far away felt the same twinges and money poured into the Duck Egg Conscience Fund, which was widely publicized. How noble of the old boys to make old Duck Egg rich. Well, not exactly.

The going rate to clean a conscience was set at 50¢ a rock. Although many admitted that the "poor old chink" should become as rich as Rockefeller, most figured their consciences could be cleaned and renewed for 50¢ or a dollar. No restrictions were placed on how Duck Egg could spent his windfall of almost $50, but he was doled out the money a little at a time to keep him from pressing his luck and gambling it away.

Duck Egg and the immigrant Chinese are long-since gone. However, the Chinese who remained in the area left a legacy of which they and their heirs can be most proud. Although few in number, they persevered against great odds and gradually overcame the many obstacles placed in their way by narrow-minded prejudices and xenophobia. When the courts ruled in 1885 that Chinese could attend public schools, the younger generations excelled as students, became more Americanized, and eventually took their rightfully earned places as leading professionals, businessmen, and respected citizens.

The Bonanza Market, owned and operated by the Jack Bing Yok Company, is a good example of local Chinese enterprise. Here you can find everything you need in the latest lines of grits and groceries, fish bait and fresh meat, along with a charming and exotic selection of recent Chinese imports.

The Fire King and the Household Queen

The Fire King and the Household Queen

ALTHOUGH GOLD MINERS WERE ROUGH, tough, and ready, so were local businessmen—and stubborn to boot.

By July 1852 Nevada City had seven large hotels downtown, and others scattered about the surrounding countryside. All were busy. Some of the miners had built log cabins and huts and settled down with wives and families, and the general moral character of the city had improved: fewer drunks, fewer fights, and a higher tone in society—all due to the influence of "correct" female society. That's what A. A. Sargent claimed, and if you can't believe a man destined to become a historian, lawyer, congressman, and diplomat, whom can you believe?

Still, all was not tea and toast. Although the maturing miners had run out of a little roar, they could still raise hell when the mood or the booze hit. By 1855, enough drinking and fighting went on to keep 79 retail liquor houses and 18 lawyers busy, large crowds of spectators entertained, the county jail and city calaboose jammed, and the local newspapers filled with frequent items about disputes over cards, women, and refusals to serve drinks to "tanked" customers. The vast arsenal of weapons included fists, heads, feet, fingers, shotguns, pistols, hatchets, shovels, bowie knives, bar stools, and beer mugs.

When a discussion at the Nevada Restaurant over a change on a business sign shattered the silence of Commercial Street in 1857, a large crowd quickly gathered to watch the combatants pitch in with decanters, pitchers, and bar fixtures. The results were battered faces, bloody shirts, and the dissolution of another partnership. Owners and locations of local businesses changed frequently. Personality conflicts were the cause of some; King Fire, the cause of most.

King Fire wiped out large sections of Nevada City almost yearly from 1851 to 1860 except when he moved over to smite French Corral in '54, gave the county a fire break in '57, and returned to redo Rough and Ready in '59 before he returned his attention to Nevada City again in '60, '63, and '80. In his spare time, he wiped out parts of Grass Valley five times, North San Juan and Truckee four times, and Moore's Flat, You Bet, and Red Dog twice. Once was enough for Little York.

Unlike the legend, Nevada City didn't have centuries between burns; however, each time the Fire King swept through, the city rose from the ashes faster than a flying Phoenix. Each time she was declared to be more beautiful and more substantial as more and more buildings were built of "fireproof" brick.

How fast could she rise? In the days before indoor plumbing, electrical wiring, interior decorators, and building inspectors, a derelict building was torn down and a two-story eight-room frame house with a balcony was thrown up and occupied in two days.

When Nevada City again vanished in "clouds of smoke and a whirlwind of fire" in one short hour in 1856, a flock of pelicans flew over the blackened remains, spiralled down, dropped a load of fish near the gutted courthouse, then soared away. General Wulf nailed a large American flag to the charred stump of an old flag staff and offered a good smoke of cigars to passing customers. These omens suggest many things, but unflappable speculators saw only good prospects.

NEVADA CITY REAL ESTATE
IN THE NEW YORK HOTEL
MARILYN STARKEY

In 1857, the one year the Fire King spared Nevada City, the Monumental Hotel and other buildings along Deer Creek were swept away by a flood when a reservoir broke. Although maintaining a hotel under such fire and water circumstances was a monumental headache, hotels and boarding houses in Nevada City once numbered 24. Among them was the New York Hotel, which opened for business in 1853, was wiped out to the tune of $7,000 in the fire of '56, then rebuilt and offered for sale in '57 as a great bargain at reduced prices. The owner wanted to return to the more sedate Atlantic states. Mrs. Adams, formerly of the What Cheer House, took over the New York in '57, and in '58 the hotel burned again to the tune of $4,000. The price had gone down, but the hotel went up again and burned again in '63 along with all the hotels, restaurants, fire houses, the courthouse, and most of the churches.

The New York Hotel was rebuilt, destroyed by fire again in 1880, and rebuilt, bigger and better, with two stories. The dedication of the new hotel was followed by a grand ball.

Gradually, hotels in Nevada City dwindled. Their undoing was not the Fire King but the Household Queen. As more wives and families settled into their own little cottages and Victorian showplaces, hotel trade fell off, and hotels were transformed into shops and offices—just as the New York Hotel is today.

If It's Not White, It's Black

If It's Not White, It's Black

OF ALL THE SAD TRUTHS in the history of Nevada County, one of the saddest was the general prejudice against any color of skin other than white, and some of the whites and near-whites, such as the Irish, Greeks, and Italians, were not particularly popular. Indians, Chinese, Mexicans, and blacks were treated with contempt at best and downright cruelty at worst.

The peaceful Nisenan Indians were eliminated by either white man's diseases or bullets or simply shoved aside to campoodies in outlying regions or to reservations in other parts of the state. By the great white father's law, some of these native American "children" were required to carry passports when entering white settlements, and no white man could be convicted of any crime solely on the testimony of an Indian. Of what use was a "Digger" who scrabbled in the dirt and ate roots and bulbs and didn't appreciate the value of the gold he trod on? Move 'em out. By 1870 only nine Indians were listed in the Nevada County census.

Although Mexico also had some legitimate claims to California, the Anglos simply flexed their muscles, raised the Bear Flag over the California Republic, and took the land. Mexicans who remained and staked out mining claims were denounced as breeders of violence and vice and potential Joaquin Murieta "greasers" who dabbled in human gore. These foreign menaces were simply taxed out of existence by the Foreign Miners' Tax of 1850, which demanded they each pay $20 a month for the pleasure of digging in the land that once was theirs. Most soon left the area.

The blacks who were brought to California as slaves were given their freedom—freedom to work for slave wages as miners or menials under the guidance and protection of their white caretakers. Although blacks were considered to be sexually promiscuous and not very bright, they were so few their foibles were tolerated with amusement. What harm could they do? They couldn't vote, serve on juries, or testify in any court action involving whites.

Of all the prejudices, great and small, the Chinese were the most sinned against—while doing a little sinning.

Chinese laborers were generally tolerated during the most difficult and dangerous part of the construction of the Central Pacific Railroad through the Sierra Nevada in the 1860s and later on the Nevada County Narrow Gauge Railroad in the 1870s. The Chinese were said to be more reliable and harder workers than the Irish, and they worked for a pittance. However, after the hard work was done and the Chinese began to compete for jobs fit for white workers, they were tolerated no more. "The Chinese must go!" became the battle cry—by "lawful means," of course.

Through some convoluted legal thinking, Chinese were declared to be blacks, based on the simple color code that what was not white was black. This gave the Chinese the same rights as Indians and blacks—essentially none.

The Chinese could not hold land and could work no mining claim unless it was so poor that no white man wanted it. The Foreign Miners' Tax, which had been repealed, was reinstated. Chinese were required to pay first $3 and then $4 per month per person. In addition a ship's captain had to pay a large tax for each Chinese he imported into the U.S. These

~GALLERY:
NEVADA CITY, CALIFORNIA
SING LEE'S CHINESE LAUNDRY 1882
MARILYN STARKEY

were some of the legal means used to keep Chinese out and to get them to leave. Some did leave, but many couldn't afford the passage back to China.

To the chagrin of the whites, some of the Chinese worked the essentially worthless claims and paid the exorbitant tax. However, most Chinese worked as domestics and cooks, operated laundries, grew and peddled fruits and vegetables, or became businessmen in local Chinatowns. When anti-Chinese clubs formed and persuaded whites to dismiss all Chinese employees or have their business boycotted, out went the Chinese, slowly but surely.

The Chinese were blamed for everything from missing chickens to burning towns, and sometimes they were guilty. They did love chickens and were not above lifting a few from their roosts to roast, and they did build sections of tinderbox shops and houses in Grass Valley, Nevada City, and Truckee. Those Chinatowns did occasionally go up in flames at the drop of a spark and take the towns with them. Each time a chicken was stolen or a Chinatown went up in smoke, white citizens agitated to get them further out of town—or better yet—out of the county, out of the state, and back to China. Truckee succeeded with mixed results.

The Chinese reigned supreme in one trade—washing whites' dirty linen. When the whites of Truckee tried to drive the Chinese out of that trade by establishing a white-operated laundry, the laundry proved to be a white elephant, and whites were forced to send their dirty duds to Reno or Sacramento. Apparently white ladies were above such menial tasks.

Then, a great white hope appeared on the horizon, a self-proclaimed laundryman, who took Truckee in. When he had gathered enough dirty linen to open a clothing store somewhere—somewhere other than Truckee—he packed up and left, leaving Truckee shirtless and shiftless.

Caught between a wife who refused to do laundry and a pile of dirty linen, prominent citizens who proclaimed publically "The Chinese must go!" became closet patrons of Chinese washhouses.

Local Chinatowns and most of the local Chinese are no more. At this location on Commercial Street, the Sing Lee Chinese Laundry was one of the last establishments—before the Laundromats—to wash the whites' dirty linen. Now, it is a coffee house and art gallery where artists show the best faces of historic, picturesque Nevada County.

A Borrower and a Lender Be

A Borrower and a Lender Be

IN THE ISOLATED, news-hungry gold-country setting, newspapers flourished even in the smallest and remotest mining camps. By 1851, Nevada County had its first newspaper, the *Nevada Journal*, which was the second newspaper published in the gold camps. By 1880, fifteen different newspapers had been published, daily, weekly, tri-weekly, semi-monthly, and semi-occasionally for longer and shorter times in Nevada County. The going rate for newspapers ranged from 10 to 50 cents, which was only slightly less expensive than an early guidebook to the gold fields and only slightly more reliable.

Since the harried editor-publisher-reporter of most local newspapers was often hard put to find hard news to fill space, he filled it with letters to the editor along with so-so poetry, self-righteous sermons, political diatribes, cultural essays, and anecdotes either written by himself or sent in by his readers. These and brief pieces of local, national, and international news were scattered around advertisements and legal notices, which filled most of the space as these paid the bills. Readers had to be sharp to distinguish the so-called news from personal opinions, put-ons, and put-downs. Editors were highly political and highly opinionated, and they expressed both freely—sometimes to their regret.

In the good old days before lawsuits reigned supreme—although they were not unknown—a disgruntled reader who took exception to an editor's or correspondent's comments wouldn't sue, he would simple try to knock a different opinion into the offender's head or shoot him and end their differences.

Even though it was not without its dangers,

becoming a published writer was relatively easy. Both newspapers and magazines opened their pages to unknowns, and that's how some California writers began their literary careers. Authorship was not limited to males only. Some of the best letters about the early days written by Dame Shirley Clappe were published in the Marysville *Herald* and signed simply, "Shirley."

Although local newspapers multiplied, eastern and foreign newspapers remained scarce and relatively expensive in remote areas. To satiate the miners' hunger for news from home, Hamlet Davis came up with a simple, profitable solution. In 1850, he decided to a borrower and a lender be. You could borrow and he would lend—for a fee. He opened a reading room in an upstairs section of his store in Nevada City where for a fee you could read outdated eastern and California newspapers.

Since Grass Valley and Nevada City were among the first, largest, and richest gold-rush mining camps—and never ghosted, completely—they were the subject of many letters, journals, newspapers, and histories, early and late, that told and retold the rushers' story.

As early as 1855, a local newspaper started publishing the history of Nevada County, which was only officially four years old. A string of city directories that contained brief histories followed after. Tome after tome of the history of California a la Bancroft and Hittell also found ready readers. In many of these county histories, if you paid a fee of about $100, you could get your "mug" included along with a brief biography. However, in the 1880 history of Nevada County, "mugs" of local residents were replaced with sketches of

PUBLIC LIBRARY

NEVADA
CITY
PUBLIC
LIBRARY
ORIG. 1857
PRESENT LIBRARY
1907

OFFICE
M. HELLING

NEVADA CITY PUBLIC LIBRARY
MARILYN STARKEY

businesses, homes, ranches, mining operations, and other scenes enlivened with generic children, dogs, elegant strollers, and dashing riders.

Local authors, meaning anyone who lived here for a few months or a few years, such as "Old Block" (Alonzo Delano) and "Yellow Bird" (John Rollin Ridge), cashed in on the demand for books about California by California transplants.

In a relatively short time, reminiscences and romanticized short stories and books about the good old days became popular. In 1888, a local editor commented that Bret Harte, the author of "An Heiress of Red Dog," should go look at the solitary remaining building upon the rugged and desolate site of the old camp and fall down on his knees and worship his imaginative powers. Red Dog was long-since dead, but the demand for gold-rush history lived on, and still does.

Although local bookstores had circulating libraries, avid readers demanded more. In January 1860 a letter to the editor outlined a plan that was working but needed more public support. For an initial fee of $5.00 and a monthly fee of 50¢, a person could join the Library Association, which had been formed in 1858 in Nevada City with 100 members and about 300 books to supply the wants and raise the intellectual status of the community. Although the Association had increased their holdings to 1,000 books, membership had dropped. Many potential members had rushed off to Washoe. The Association needed more members so they could buy more books so members could partake of the purest, noblest, and most satisfying of human enjoyments—reading a good book. Though living in the midst of poverty in a cabin, a good book could give more pleasures than could be bought by the ignorant owners of the richest mine in California (or Washoe!)—or so the writer claimed.

Thus, reading rooms and library associations came to Nevada County early. By 1898, even Chalk Bluff had a Literary Society to which reportedly everyone on the bluff belonged except Jerry Goodwin, superintendent of the You Bet gold mine.

Then, through a Carnegie Foundation endowment granted in 1904, this Nevada City public library was built and dedicated in 1907. Through these doors pass nearly 1,000 readers a week who can check out thousands of books for absolutely free. Within the walls of this library is one of the richest gold-rush treasures to be found anywhere—local newspapers that report Nevada County's history almost from its beginning. Here, all the best—and some of the worst—gold-rush events and writings await readers who want to dig in and sort the grit from the gold.

Neither Indian, nor Chief, nor Crazy

Neither Indian, nor Chief, nor Crazy

O F ALL THE "GIN MILLS" in Nevada City, the Chief Crazy Horse Inn comes closest to exuding the ambience and the smell of an early-day no-holds-barred bar.

Consider the name. In the early days, names signified little more than the largess of the owner's overactive imagination. Hotels were humble huts, emporiums were stick stores, and restaurants were canvas tents. Names were suspect. So it is with the Chief Crazy Horse Inn. The proprietor is neither Indian, nor chief, nor certifiably crazy—except like a fox. The only Inn about the establishment is that is an "in" place to go for those who like their bars dim, their whiskey straight, their conversations loud, and their clothes casual.

In contrast to other local bars that have succumbed to the Marin fern-bar syndrome, the Chief displays in his Inn—which claims also to be a "Museum" so children can be allowed—a magnificent collection of Indian baskets and rugs covered with a layer of historical dust dating back to who knows when.

With those artifacts and that name, the Chief is not at all like early day name-droppers. No profit-respecting barkeep would name a bar after an Indian—Chief, Crazy, or not. Indians were not in favor. Just because the Nisenans were first on the land in Nevada County, didn't mean they had any rights to the land. Not when white miners wanted it. Whites soon made Indians scarce. They simply shot or hanged them or moved them first outside of the city and then outside of the county. About the only thing they didn't move out was the Indian medicine rock, which remains on the outskirts of Nevada City. It was probably too big to move.

Even if a barkeep could scare up an Indian for a potential customer, it was against the law to sell him liquor. Naming a bar after a group who could not patronize you would be truly crazy.

Although the Chief's Inn is rather unorthodox, it has historical precedents. In the early days, you couldn't tell a saloon by its name; in most, you could get more than a drink; and most barkeeps had a gimmick.

You couldn't cash a check at the Bank Exchange, but you probably could find several councilmen, unofficially, at The Council Chamber. Both were saloons.

Dave Ashmore ran a combination saloon and Spanish dance house; the Opera Saloon advertised a marble-bed billiard table and a reading room with the latest papers; and one bar had a ten pin alley. The Union saloon had an oyster saloon in the basement and proudly proclaimed: "No Chinese employed in the House." While one saloon advertised Gilt Edge beer for "family use," another served "elegant refreshments for the inner man."

As early as 1851 a band played night and day at Barker's Exchange as from 500 to 1,000 miners crowded into the bar where many tried their luck—which was usually bad—at 15 gambling tables. Another saloon had a most rare and unfailing gimmick—the young, then-pretty Madame "Moustache" Dumont who charmed the miners even as she pocketed their pokes while dealing them twenty-two in a game of twenty-one.

At the Rialto, Dick Gray, alias "Liberal Dick," served rum punch, brandy punch, and an occasional punch on the head "on short notice." Punches on the head were frequent in

CHIEF CRAZY HORSE INN
COMMERCIAL STREET, NEVADA CITY
MARILYN STARKEY

most bars and a popular form of entertainment.

In the early days, several thousand of the boys poured out of the saloons to cheer on Frank Cleveland and "Curly" during a two-hour rough and tumble fight on Main Street in broad daylight. As the town became more civilized, an officer stopped a brawl in which two combatants "heeled" with three-legged bar stools beat each other over the head. Bystanders complained because the fight was just about to get interesting.

Sometimes the law was more compassionate. When Dr. McNaulton, a half-crazy dentist who practiced in local bars, got into a fistic discussion with John Smith, they were both arrested and fined $8. Since the Dr. was broke, the law officer towed him from saloon to saloon so he could collect from his patients and pay his fine. Soon after, the Dr. hit a nerve when he was hired to treat a fellow drinker's sore lip and decided to yank a tooth to boot. In payment, the ungrateful patient pounded the Dr.'s teeth into the barroom floor.

The well-known barkeep "Blaze" not only capitalized on the patronage of the dependably thirsty pillars of local justice, he lured in customers with exhibits of rattlesnakes, mountain quail, the first litter of kittens and the first Japanese goldfish in the county, a pair of hand-reared hummingbirds, a "humungous" cabbage, a Southern shoe from a Civil War battlefield, and a thieving magpie that carried off anything it could get in its beak, including a piece of type from the newspaper office.

The pace in Nevada City saloons was always fast. When some of the boys thirsty for a little action uncaged two foxes in the presence of a pack of city hounds, one fox sought sanctuary in the St. Louis Hotel where the hounds caught him out and did him in. The other charged through a cigar store, strewing cheroots in his wake, and then decided to go to Blaze's—perhaps in search of justice. With the hounds in hot pursuit, the fox mounted the bar and grinned defiance at both the bellowing Blaze and the bugling hounds. Since no knight of the bar came to his defense, the case of the fox on the town-o was soon closed.

Gone are the mines and most of the miners. Gone are the Indians and many of the jackasses. Gone are the hurdy-gurdy houses, the billiard saloons, and Madame Moustache.

Also gone is the reign of the Fire King. Before he departed in '63, he left Nevada City once again in a pile of ashes that acted as "guano" that nourished the rapid growth of the new city. The Chief's, along with most of the buildings on Commercial Street that now hustle each other and the tourist trade, grew from that guano.

As it was in the beginning, so it was in '63. One of the most lucrative professions in the new and improved Nevada City was still barkeeping. So it is today. But as time passed, along with most of the native Indians and a few prejudices, what was "out" came "in." People feigned fascination with Indian culture and everyone went "native" over Indian baskets, jewelry, and clothing. Once it became profitable, Indian culture was allowed to return to Nevada City even though most of the Indian items for sale locally are imported from the southwest. Today, a German-Spanish-Basque proprietor transformed into a Crazy Indian Chief is "heap" good business.

Same Name, Same Game; Fair Play
With No Gouging

Same Name, Same Game; Fair Play With No Gouging

SAM BRANNAN, an early California entrepreneur, had the right basic idea. One of the surest ways to make a quick profit during the gold rush was to corner the market on a "necessity," buy cheap, and sell dear to the rushers as they rushed by. Sam made his first fortune selling 20¢ gold pans for $16.

Others soon caught on and prices of scarce commodities skyrocketed. In '49, bread that sold for 6¢ a loaf in New York sold for 75¢ in San Francisco. In local mining camps, flour, pork, and mouldy biscuits went for $5 a pound. The earliest miners, who were gouging placer gold out of the earth at the rate of about $75 a day, could afford to pay.

As miners spread out in remote areas, merchants with long strings of mules loaded with provisions trod right behind. Neither the merchants nor the miners gave any thought to establishing permanent towns. Their only thoughts were to make their fortunes quickly and return home. Since the most profitable businesses provided the bare necessities of mining supplies, food, booze, entertainment, and shelter, makeshift gambling halls, stores, saloons, restaurants, and hotels soon spread out around rich diggings. When the placer diggin's along Deer Creek proved to be some of the richest, a crude settlement began to form. That was the beginning of Nevada City, one of the few mining camps that never ghosted, although she grew pale and wan at times.

In the early years, while prospectors pockmarked her face, Nevada City was no beauty, but when it was discovered her beauty went deep, deep into rich hard-rock mines, it lured in large capital investors and a stable labor force. She also had other charms. Her timber and water resources attracted entrepreneurs who formed large companies to supply the nearby mines and developing communities with building materials and power. Her fertile soils seduced farmers, orchardists, and ranchers who came to grow food for the growing population. All this, in turn, pulled in artisans, professionals, and businesses to provide more than just the bare necessities. Commercialism was the name of the game, and, in general, it paid. The more it paid, the more attractive, settled, and prosperous Nevada City became.

Soon, the howl of the coyote was replaced by the buzz of the saw, the bang of the hammer, the rumble of merchant and mining carts, and the humbug of sales pitches. Although young Nevada City was still no raving beauty, she had an attractive variety of goods and services to offer.

In the early 1850s, at the Deer Creek Bakery, you could buy bread, pies, and liquors. At the Western Market, you could buy groceries and liquors. At the Milk Depot, you could buy milk and liquor; milk for 50¢ a quart and milk punch for 25¢ a glass.

You could get your watch or pistol repaired, have a nugget crafted into a fancy piece of jewelry, buy a pair of miner's hobnailed boots, and get a liquor-laced elixir from several physicians. Stores advertised fair play with no gouging, and some would deliver free within six miles of the city.

At the City Bath House they would launder your clothes and stick them in pigeonholes so when you came in from the diggin's you could bathe and change for a night on the town.

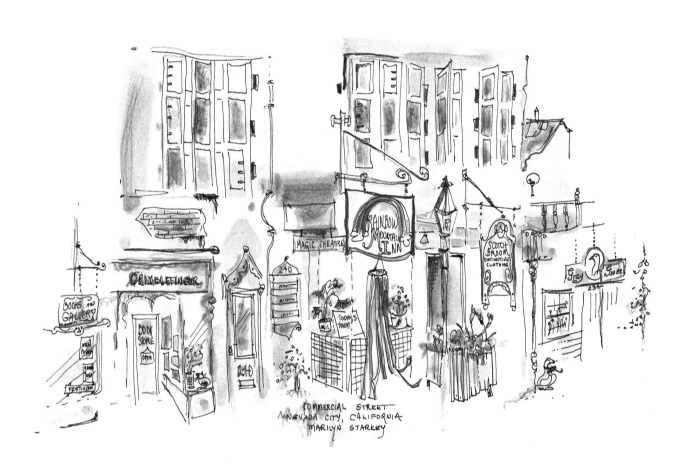

COMMERCIAL STREET
NEVADA CITY, CALIFORNIA
MARILYN STARKEY

The city was getting a little class. Ordinances removed all slaughterhouses to at least 1½ miles outside the city limits, ordered downtown property owners to build plank sidewalks, and banned cattle and pigs from mixing with city pedestrians.

In 1859, when many of the miners rushed off to the Washoe silver area, Nevada City grew pale and wan, and prices took a nosedive. However, the basic needs of the quick and the dead were still supplied.

You could book passage on the Nevada and Washoe Saddle Train over the Henness Pass to Virginia City for $20, payable in advance. The People's Stage line would take you for $15.

The Italian Barber would keep a watchful eye on your precious head and give you a shave for a quarter and a shampoo for 50¢. At the Sign of the Padlock you could buy stoves, tinware, hardware, rope, hydraulic pipes, tools, and cutlery. You could buy ice cream over the U.S. Bakery, and rent horses and carriages at two nearby livery stables. T. M. Wood, who specialized in "taking children," claimed he could take their photograph in less than a second in any kind of weather. He would also preserve an image of the deceased in a most appropriate manner.

Undertaker William Groves had a new hearse, would undertake on the shortest notice, and would not be outdone—or underdone—in prices. Small coffins ranged from $3 to $10; and large, from $10 to $20. Just leave your orders at the carpenter shop.

At the numerous dry goods stores you could buy French prints, silk mantillas, chantilly veils, and China silk dresses for $7.50 and up, along with velvet and Brussels carpets and damask curtains.

Dr. Levason, a dentist, could be found upstairs next to the meat market. His fees were $2.50 for each operation, the same as in "the States."

Prices were right at the Cheap Refreshment Saloon, and A. Rosenthal would cut and fit plain and fancy cassimeres and broadcloth at reasonable rates. Cheap John's promised to undersell anyone in clothing, books, and notions, and the Rudolph & Hunt Drug Store sold cheaper than the cheapest.

Today, on the same narrow and crooked streets of Nevada City, stores with imaginative names play the same commercial game with a few changes. Alpha Hardware, one of the longest operating businesses in Nevada County has been "poshed" up, and the crockery store has been replaced by the Nevada City Crystal & Glass shop. Miners' hobnailed boots have been replaced with Birkenstock sandals at Love Your Feet or ersatz Indian moccasins at the Sitting Bull Leather Company. Milliners and dressmakers have been replaced by the Small Town Clothier, Scarlet Belle, Mountain Song, M'Lady's, and Scotch Broom. At the Button Works, you won't find buttons of bone and shell but metal buttons that tell the world what you think, whether the world wants to read it or not.

You can still find some of the bare necessities at the Country Rose Cafe, Rainbow Mountain Inn, Friar Tuck's, Mine Shaft, Citizen's Pizza, Apple Fare, Cirino's, McGee's, Selaya's, Posh Nosh, El Bandito, and the Chief Crazy Horse Inn. You can also find a variety of those non-essentials dear to the tourist trade at Osborn and Woods, Gray Goose, Top Drawer, Herb Shop, and the Third Whale.

In the old days, the Fire King wiped out many businesses; today, the fickle taste of the tourist trade makes or breaks. The trades that pay, stay; but what is here today could be gone tomorrow. Meanwhile, they all welcome you and your charge card.

48

Justice Dispensed at the Bar,
or Go to Blaze's

Justice Dispensed at the Bar, or Go to Blaze's

IN THE EARLIEST GOLD-RUSH DAYS, there were no courts, no jailers, and no jails; however, there was a form of miners' justice. The basic law of the land was self-defense. You had a right to defend yourself and your property. Under that law, disputes were settled quickly and sometimes permanently with fists, knives, or guns. If the fight was considered to be fair, one-on-one, face-to-face, with no bushwhacking, the one who walked away with the least damages was the winner. Even if the loser paid with his life, there was no appeal to a higher court.

Theft was considered to be a more heinous crime than murder most foul, and punishment was swift and sure if not always just, as the prejudices and passions of the miners ruled. When a suspect was brought before a miners' court, he was tried, sentenced, and punished—all within a few hours. The accused was usually found guilty and taken to the nearest tree and either stripped and severely whipped, branded, and banished—or hanged. When Nevada County was part of Yuba County and the county seat was at far-away Marysville, local miners' courts, which took little time and even less expense, rid the community of several suspected thieves and murderers. The general opinion was that most of them were probably guilty. If not guilty of the specific crime for which they were tried, the miners felt they deserved to be punished on the general principal that the camp was better off without them.

When boundaries were redrawn in 1851 and Nevada County was formed with Nevada City as the county seat, lawyers rushed in with great expectations of fat fees and quick prestige. They were not disappointed. As Judge Lynch gradually gave way to the legal judicial system, lawyers worked the rich fields of lawsuits that resulted from the exuberant behavior of the boys that when enhanced by booze frequently erupted in fistic discussions, name-calling contests, shoot-outs, brawls, murders, and mayhem. The rivalry for the attention of the few women in the camp resulted in broken hearts, broken heads, and lawsuits. Arguments over stolen pigs, cows, mules, pokes, and wives along with disputes over cards, drinks, property lines, unpaid debts, and who was the orneriest cuss in town filled court dockets and lawyers' pockets. In addition, litigation over mining claims and water rights sometimes went on for years as the cases were carried through the court system. Lawyers who worked these legal bonanzas not only had steady employment but the golden opportunity to gain prestige in the judicial and political arenas, which were closely linked.

Soon, lawyers became almost as numerous as saloon keepers and were among their most consistent clientele. With the help of booze and lawyers, justice slowed down and became more expensive. In 1851 when a mining case was tried in Si Brown's saloon in Rough and Ready, both parties agreed that the loser would pay for all court costs including all the liquor drunk by the court, jury, lawyers, witnesses, and bystanders. As soon as court was in session, they all began to drink. The more they drank, the longer the trial. Late in the night, the jury retired with a bottle of whiskey to deliberate. With the dawn, they were found

COMMERCIAL STREET
NEVADA CITY, CALIFORNIA
MARILYN STARKEY

strewn around town. Since no verdict had been reached, it was declared a mistrial; and according to the rules, the plaintiff paid all costs, which amounted to $1,400 of which $1,200 was the liquor bill.

The first real courthouse was not much—a shabby little building covered with red cloth. When a mob of miners was thwarted by Judge Caswell in their attempt to hang a gambler for shooting a miner, some of the mob suggested they hang the judge instead. They didn't, and the legal system scored a point. The gambler was tried in the Red Courthouse and acquitted. Justice scored another point when a mob in Grass Valley wanted to hang a man suspected of being an incendiary on the general principal that Nevada City had hanged a man and Grass Valley should hang one, too. Cooler heads prevailed, and the suspect was tried and released.

As lawyers increased and lawsuits multiplied, a new courthouse was built on the site of the present courthouse. Before the first trial could be held in 1856, Nevada City and the new courthouse lay in ashes, and a petition was circulated requesting the county seat be moved to Grass Valley. Nevada City held onto her seat, the courthouse was rebuilt, reburned in 1863, and rebuilt.

Not far away from the site of these courthouses was another historic landmark, Blaze's saloon, which ironically was one of the few buildings to defy the Fire King in 1863. Here, John Bazley, "Blaze," a barkeep with style and imagination, advertised: "Want a good drink, Go to Blaze's." After a hard day of dispensing justice at the bar, lawyers and judges often did just that, as Blaze's was an easy walk downhill from the courthouse. Sometimes, a lawyer flushed with victory would treat all parties and "hangers on" to drinks at Blaze's.

On a cold winter evening when a poor fellow who was ailing with the matrimony mania couldn't get a license to wed a "frail" (because it was Sunday and the clerk's office was closed), the boys at Blaze's did the best they could. After Blaze poured a round of drinks and spouted some mumbo-jumbo legalese over the groom, the boys pasted a big red seal on a poll-tax receipt, pronounced it a marriage certificate, pinned it on the groom's coat, and sent him on his way to marital bliss. Much later, as the boys wended their way home they passed the groom, who was standing in the rain outside the bride's bolted door declaring she was legally his and he would remain on her doorstep until she took him in. Little did he know, he had been taken in.

Lawyers in those good old days settled cases, both in and out of court, with legal double talk or any other weapon at hand. During a loud dispute in a saloon, a gambler did his best to kill a local judge. A lawyer, who slept nearby, heard the ruckus, rushed out of bed in his red flannels, grabbed a large stick, charged into the fray, felled the gambler with one bonk on the head, and zipped back to bed leaving everyone to ponder: Who was that red router?

Although you can no longer go to Blaze's, you can still go to court; and there are plenty of local lawyers willing to take you there. The courthouse with its 1937 Art Moderne facade—sometimes disparagingly called WPA Gothic—still stands sentinel over Nevada City. Around lunch time, lawyers and other legal and local dignitaries can be found gathered at the corner of Pine and Commercial discussing important issues such as whether an impertinent white or a sassy red would best enhance the haute cuisine served at the Country Rose Cafe—where Blaze and the boys once dispensed justice and booze.

Lola and Historical Hype

HERE LIVED LOLA, the lady of many names and dubious fame, who was born Marie Dolores Eliza Rosanna Gilbert in Limerick, Ireland, on 3 July 1818. Lola, who despite her mediocre acting and dancing, became the toast and the scandal of three continents and defied writers' warehouses of words to describe her charm. Lola, the divine, eccentric, wild, wanton, willful, captivating, fabulous, flamboyant, tempestuous, scandalous, headstrong, fiery, life-lover, husband-and-lover collector, and darling of historians—male historians, especially.

How fitting that this little reconstructed cottage, which was once the home of Lola who knew so well how to hype herself, now houses the Nevada County Chamber of Commerce, which knows so well how to hype the history of the lovely Lola and our paradisaic county.

Unlike Lola's meteoric career when it blazed brightly in Europe, her short spurt of fireworks in Nevada County was like a small skyrocket, up with a flash and down like a stick.

At the age of 19, Dolores refused to marry "a gouty old rascal" and eloped with a young army officer. Soon after, her young husband rode off with a lady friend. Dolores cried a little, laughed a little, and decided to become a famous dancer.

After studying in Madrid, she debuted in London as the mysterious Spanish dancer, Lola Montez. From London, Lola whirled on to perform her somewhat shocking Spider Dance across Europe. While stomping out imaginary spiders, she collected such lovers and admirers as Franz Liszt, Alexandre Dumas, Victor Hugo, and Honoré de Balzac.

When King Ludwig I of Bavaria became acquainted with Lola's body beautiful, he built her a villa and luscious Lola was transformed into the Countess of Landsfeld. In return, the Countess dabbled in politics, became involved in a revolution, and to avoid arrest removed her royal presence to London. There Lola married again and soon had to leave England to avoid being arrested for bigamy. Unforgettable Lola had forgotten that she didn't have a proper divorce from her first husband.

In 1851, Lola brought her act to the United States. Her first performance in San Francisco in May 1853 was a sellout. But seeing the captivating Lola perform once seemed to be enough. As attendance fell, Lola picked up another "husband," Patrick Hull, and moved on to greener audiences in Sacramento, Marysville, Grass Valley, and Nevada City.

Lola and Pat's arrival in Grass Valley, July 1853, created a hubbub that is still heard clearly by many locals. Regular admission prices were doubled, and Lola played to boisterous, jam-packed audiences. The deafening 24-hour crunching of the surrounding gold-stamp mills was reportedly drowned out by their thunderous applause. Once again, once was enough. The audience was so small at one performance, Lola canceled the show and settled down to a normal Lola-life.

She bought this simple cottage on Mill Street from Gilmore Meredith and frequently orchestrated Parisian-style salons for the local gentry, mine owners, visiting musicians, performers, investors, and business people—all male. During these parties, Lola passed out some passable cigars and booze, sang a few foreign songs, danced her famous Spider Dance, told interesting stories, and showed her collection

M. STARKEY

LOLA MONTEZ' HOME: 1853-1855
NEVADA COUNTY CHAMBER OF COMMERCE
GRASS VALLEY, CALIFORNIA

of admirers her menagerie of canaries, dogs, sheep, a goat, horse, wild cat, parrot, lamb, and grizzly bear.

During her stay in Nevada County, Lola also took a pack trip to Truckee Meadow, rode a sleigh into Nevada City and threw a few snowballs, fell off her horse while picking wild flowers, threw a little Christmas party for some small girls, and was bitten by her chained grizzly bear, which was promptly sold for bull bait. In the process, Lola grew tired of "Hully wedlock" and applied for a divorce.

Lola may or may not have taught little Lotta Crabtree, who lived up Mill Street, a few dances and encouraged her to perform on an anvil in Rough and Ready. She definitely did

try to horsewhip editor Henry Shipley for reprinting some unkind remarks about her and her European friends. The entire episode happened a few blocks away in the Golden Gate Saloon where the Holbrooke Hotel now stands. Lola complained that she was forced to use her riding whip, which had never been used on the back of a horse, to whip an "Ass."

Lola left Grass Valley in May 1855 never to return. In 1856 she sold her cottage, retired from the stage, and earned her living by giving how-to-keep-your-beauty lectures in New York, where she died on 17 January 1864. After more than 125 years, tourists still flock to see where Lola lived and kept her bear.

A Hard Day's Night

A Hard Day's Night

AFTER STANDING KNEE-DEEP in near freezing water as they dug, dumped, and washed yards of rock and dirt through "Rube Goldberg" gold-catching gadgets, all that most of the young, hardy 49ers wanted at the end of a hard day's work was food, booze, and a bed. During good weather, they would soothe their rumbling bellies with a load of hardtack and "bug-chowder" flavored with salt pork and washed down with ache-bustin', mind-dullin', tanglefoot whiskey. They would then roll out their blanket—two if they were well-to-do—under a tree and dream of making their pile and tromping home triumphant before the first snow fell.

Those dreams came true for only a few. When the cold, relentless rains came and the snow blew, most of the miners hied to the valleys to wait for spring. Others scurried to spend a hard day's night in the makeshift canvas and shake boarding houses and hotels that quickly sprang up around the placer mining camps.

In these early ticky-tacky structures, the booze and food were passable and the beds impossible. Some rented floor space where for a dollar a night a "guest" could throw down his blanket and sleep snore-to-snore and exchange ubiquitous litters of lice and flocks of fleas. Others provided narrow bunks nailed to walls where the "great hairy unwashed" were stacked like cords of wood. Peace and privacy were not to be had at any price, as partitions, if any, were of canvas or cloth.

As early as April 1851, Grass Valley boasted the Grass Valley Hotel and the Grass Valley Farmers Hotel. Class distinction seemed to be settling in, and improvements were being made. The Illinois Hotel added a second story, the Missouri Hotel was enlarged, and the Beatty Hotel added a new front and a piazza.

Among these early hotels were the roots of the Holbrooke Hotel, whose history is out front and set in cement on two bronze plaques. According to which plaque you're reading, first came the Golden Gate Saloon in 1851 or 1852, to which was added The Exchange Hotel in 1853.

Here in 1854 the fiery Lola Montez blazed into the saloon, where the alcoholic newspaper editor Henry Shipley could usually be found, and tried to horsewhip him for giving her some bad press. The wooden structure withstood that historic blaze but was destroyed by fire in September 1855 and rebuilt of brick.

Although little can be said in favor of the dreaded, destructive Fire King, who repeatedly wiped out tinderbox structures, he did force the construction of more fireproof and attractive brick buildings. After the Fire King smacked down most of Grass Valley, including the Exchange Hotel, in June 1862, the present structure was built.

D. P. Holbrooke bought the Exchange in 1879 and transformed it into the stately Holbrooke Hotel. In May '80, a mad bull charged down Main Street, crashed through the main entry of the Holbrooke, and headed toward the dining room before a brave torero stopped the charge and forced the bull out backwards. In his wake, the bull left damaged walls, broken glass, and a room decorated with what looked like green paint, but wasn't.

Soon after, on a sunny Sunday morning, a sheep broke away from a flock being driven through town, jumped through a window into

HISTORIC HOLBROOKE HOTEL, 1851
GRASS VALLEY, CALIFORNIA
MARILYN STARKEY

59

the Holbrooke dining room, then gamboled out the kitchen window.

In April 1881, the first telephones in Grass Valley were installed in the Holbrooke, the Scotia Mine, and Johnston's Hardware and connected to Marysville, 35 miles away. When a group gathered at the Holbrooke to try this novel form of communication, the Marysville party rang in with songs and violin and guitar music. After the Grass Valley group answered with songs and a tinkling piano, a male with a remarkable voice burst into an impromptu song on the Scotia Mine line. Although all the music sounded like it came from a deep mine shaft, the notes were distinct and the experiment was declared an enjoyable success.

On 21 October 1897, C. H. Mackay from New York registered at the Holbrooke along with two other gentlemen named Mackay and Flood from San Francisco. Clarence Mackay's father, John W. Mackay, and James C. Flood were two of the Bonanza Kings of the Nevada Comstock Lode. By 1897 James C. Flood was dead, but his son, James L., was very much alive. The three registered names probably represented big—really big—pokes that were first filled with Washoe silver and then used to build transcontinental underwater cable and telegraph systems.

On 25 April 1898, Republican ex-President Benjamin Harrison from Indianapolis, Democratic ex-President Grover Cleveland from Buzzards Bay, ex-heavyweight boxing champion James J. Corbett from San Francisco, and heavyweight champion Robert Fitzsimmons from New York signed in. Speculation is that these political rivals came to see the rival boxers slug it out in an exhibition match. On the same date, a "Geo. Gould Jr." from New York registered. If this George was the son of Jay Gould, he was the president of six railroads and the vice president of Western Union.

During the same period two guests listed their address as the county jail.

Here, through the years, people great and ordinary signed in and slept the sleep of the just and the unjust in increasingly comfortable quarters. They gathered in front of the Holbrooke to listen to hour-long speeches by politicians; cheer the boys off to the Spanish-American War and World Wars I and II; wave the American flag during Fourth of July parades; and applaud the arrival of visiting dignitaries. Here, millions of dollars changed hands in mining and business transactions, toasts were drunk at wakes, weddings, and fancy balls, and tables groaned with sumptuous holiday feasts. As it was yesterday, so it is today. Step inside and soak up the ambiance of history.

The Good Earth

The Good Earth

GOLD! SILVER! AND SLICKENS! Those were the three siren songs that drove argonauts insane and sent them scurrying here, there, or anywhere the seductive songs were sung. Many of those who heeded the cry of Gold! in 1849 and rushed madly into Nevada County rushed madly out again in 1859 when the song of Silver! lured them over the mountains to see what they could see in Washoe. Those who stuck to their posts couldn't hear the Silver! song over the roar of their 24-hour-a-day, 7-days-a-week hydraulic monitors as they madly washed down millions of tons of gold-bearing gravel and sent acres and acres of mud, sand, and gravel called "slickens" gushing downstream to bless the farming flatlanders. The miners swore slickens were good for the farmers as anything—just anything—could be raised in those fertile remains.

Just how rich were mining slickens? When a sheep caught in a flood swam to a high knoll, the seeds that had caught in her heavy coat and been fertilized by the slickens she swam through germinated, flourished, and provided her with a movable feast until the flood water subsided. Whether that tale is true or not, slickens did eventually produce one of the biggest and bitterest court battles in the state, which, in turn, fattened up a herd of lawyers.

When winter rains and floods washed out mining debris that buried thousands of acres of farmlands, fertilized young orchards with three feet of slickens, covered millions of dollars worth of crops, and clogged rivers all the way to San Francisco Bay, ungrateful flatland farmers grew sick of too much slickens and screeched "Stop the Slickens!" The hydraulic miners turned a deaf ear until the screams got so loud they reached the ears of the federal court. In 1884, after studying a ponderous pile of legal papers—12,500 pages—Judge Lorenzo Sawyer declared it to be illegal to dump hydraulic debris into streams and rivers. That decision essentially buried all legal hydraulic mining, drove many miners out of the area, and planted the seed of an idea. Slickens and old mining claims were, indeed, good earth from which riches could be harvested after spreading some propaganda and mining the media.

At a Midwinter Fair in San Francisco, slices of locally grown oranges were floated in a bowl carved from Truckee ice to prove that crops from the tropical to the subzero were harvested in Nevada County.

By spreading glowing descriptions of the perfect weather, healthy climate, plentiful pure water, rich soil, and natural beauty of Nevada County, large tracts of land were sold to investors, who in turn sold small plots to people just lookin' for a home.

As time passed, more and more land developers and realtors cropped up and in chorus with the Chambers of Commerce sang this new siren song. New subdivisions from Chicago Park in 1887 to Alta Sierra and Lake Wildwood in the mid-20th century were the melody of their song with harmony provided by expanding commercial developments.

Those songs lured many people into the area, but few agree as to just what they heard or why they came. Many came to live and work in the towns, others to retire in subdivisions and wear snappy clothes on the golf courses. Still others, artists and artisans, pot bakers and

THE BROWNES'
CHRISTMAS TREE FARM
GRASS VALLEY, CALIFORNIA

MARILYN STARKEY

BROWNES'
TREE FARM

63

quilt makers, zealots and zanies, joined the back-to-nature stampede to do their own "thing."

Tucked away in remote parts of the county are many quaint homes and beautiful plots of ground where people like the Brownes dig away in the good earth that is a living history of the area. On the Brownes' land, Indians probably gathered acorns from the ancient oak trees and leached them in Little Greenhorn Creek. In the 1880s, an owner procured rights to 20 miner's inches of water from the stream and used it to hydraulic gold-rich gravel. Later owners got their drinking water from an abandoned hardrock mine shaft, used the stream water for irrigation, and tilled the slickens' enriched soil.

They cultivated a vineyard; nurtured a small orchard of apples, pears, prunes, walnuts, and chestnuts; lumbered the pines; raised rabbits, Louisana bullfrogs, and pieplants (rhubarb); and grazed milk cows and cattle on the verdant, irrigated permanent pasture.

In 1963, the land was sold, and the owner moved to town. Lured by siren songs praising the latest craze in California agriculture—Christmas tree plantations—the Brownes bought a part of the land, camped in an old army barracks that had been moved onto the property from Beale Air Force Base after World War II, and now dig in the good earth to grow flowers for smelling and Christmas trees for selling.

To the Cottage Bourn

To the Cottage Bourn

In Nevada County there were—and are—two types of gold deposits: placer and quartz. In placer mining, in its simplest form, water was used to wash gold-bearing soil and gravel through gold-catching devices such as pans and sluice boxes. This form of mining required a lot of water but little capital. A small group of hard workers with crude equipment could make a rich deposit pay.

In contrast, the mining methods used to extract gold from hard-rock quartz deposits were complex and required large capital investments, elaborate and costly equipment, and a large, experienced, and cheap labor force.

As surface placer deposits were worked out, some of the more adventurous and hardy miners tried their luck at hard-rock mining. Their luck was usually bad. The inexperience of the miners, the crudeness of the early machinery, and poor management led to the disastrous failure of most hard-rock mines.

Then, things began to change when tin and copper miners from Cornwall, England came to work in the gold-quartz mines. These miners, who were known as the world's greatest hard-rock miners, brought with them invaluable skills and knowledge of hard-rock mining techniques and equipment.

When the easily accessible placer deposits were picked clean by 1853 and hydraulic mining was essentially outlawed in 1884, the hard-rock quartz mines became the major source of gold production in Nevada County, one of the most productive and longest operating hard-rock gold mining areas in California and the world. Upon these hard rocks rest much of the county's historical fame.

Gold-quartz mining was a high-risk industry for both the capital investors and the miners, and only a few mines yielded high returns. The Empire mine proved to be a major exception. The slow rise but long reign of the Empire mine—from 1850 to 1956—paralleled the development of hard-rock mining in Nevada County.

Although the Empire ledge—which was discovered by George D. Roberts in 1850—produced around $3 million in gold between 1854 and 1878, it changed hands many times during the early days. In 1878 mining experts proclaimed that the mine was worked out and should be closed.

William B. Bourn, Jr., the owner's son, disagreed. After he gained control of the Empire in 1877, he reorganized. With the use of the latest mining technology and equipment, he located a rich vein of ore and hired his cousin, George W. Starr, an expert mining engineer, as mine superintendent. The Empire mine was on its way to paying the owners and investors well, very well indeed.

In over 100 years of almost continuous operation, more than $120 million in gold was taken from the Empire, the oldest, biggest, and richest gold mine in the Grass Valley mining district and one of the most famous gold-quartz mines in the world.

In 1915, a tiny 1½-ounce bar of gold produced from the ore taken from the stygian underground world of the Empire was crafted into a shiny band of gold to grace the wedding finger of the leading lady of the land, the newly-wed Mrs. Woodrow Wilson.

Although the Cornish were the major group

M STARKEY THE FRONT DOOR
AT
THE BOURN COTTAGE
EMPIRE MINE ~ GRASS VALLEY

of hard-rock miners in the area, other nationalities—for better or worse—worked in the placer and quartz mines, early and late.

In 1871, a local paper divided the miners into four simple classes—American, Irish, German, and Cornish—and jammed them into the following stereotypical pigeonholes:

The American miner is restless, not content to work for others, and can be found digging for gold in all sorts of nooks all over the world. He is exceedingly fond of telling how many fortunes he has made and lost in his colorful career of seeking color, and he will tear up the streets of Pandemonium if it will put ten cents in his pan. However, the only way to get an American miner into Heaven is to start a rumor of a gold rush in the sky.

The son of Erin is a devil-may-care miner with a heart as light as his purse. He is full of fun, generous, and kindhearted and will divide his last crumb and his last dollar with a friend. He is fond of grog, but even fonder of a good donnybrook.

The German is industrious, quiet, and usually addicted to sauerkraut, lager beer, and minding his own business. He marries early and has many children who speak German and English more or less fluently. He is a good musician and delights in smoking a meerschaum pipe and taking it easy.

The Cornish, the most skillful miner, is quiet but clannish and bullheaded. He prefers to work for others as long as he is promptly paid. He is stalwart, good-looking, and dresses better than other miners. In their leisure, Cornish miners gather around a saloon table, order a pot of ale, porter, or beer, and pass the time with stories and song. Most of them are good singers, and they are fond, very fond, of women.

These were the miners who worked the mines that made the jack that build the mansion of Bourn. Locals call it a mansion, but to Bourn it was a cottage.

In 1894 William B. Bourn, Jr. commissioned Willis Polk, a San Francisco architect, to design a cottage near the Empire mine. All in all, it is a rather nice little $30,000 cottage where Bourn would stop for short periods when he wasn't at either his San Francisco mansion or his 46-room Filoli estate in San Mateo.

Although the grounds around the cottage look somewhat like a modest English country estate, the touch of the gold country is here. The wall surrounding part of the grounds was built of rock taken from the Empire mine. In 1913, one of every native tree in California was planted on the grounds. The sprinkling system for the lawn and for fire protection is a series of small monitors. Their gigantic cousins were used in hydraulic mining operations to wash away massive hillsides.

The nearby shingled building, "The Empire Club," was once the gathering place for the socially elite—including Herbert Hoover and the King of Norway.

As many as ten gardeners once groomed the 12-acre grounds and nurtured 1,500 rose bushes and a maze of exotic and native plants and trees. However, except for special work crews, miners were not allowed on the cottage grounds.

Here, in the Empire Mine State Historic Park, visitors who come by the thousands each year can tour the miner's workplace and the capitalist's cottage—two contrasting reminders of the splendor and the reality of the past.

Rusticate and Recreate

Rusticate and Recreate

WITH THE PASSING OF THE early placer mining phase of the gold rush around 1853 and the beginning of more stable hardrock and hydraulic mining, some Nevada County mining camps transformed into villages and cities with civilized hearths and homes. Many of the young argonauts ceased their roaming and became professionals, businessmen, and miners who worked regular shifts.

No sooner had the "boys"—the majority were still under 30—settled down than they began to devise ways to get away from it all. In what little leisure they had, they got away to rusticate and recreate.

Some stuck with the tried and true, doing what they did quite well in the good old days. They drank, gambled, and caroused; and they never had to go far to find places to do it. Saloons stayed plentiful and profitable. As late as 1882 Nevada County issued licenses to 127 saloons. In '84 a local paper exaggeratedly groused that the total number of saloons was just a little less than 900.

About the only establishments that outnumbered saloons were societies. In 1879, the paper counted—again with exaggeration—about 781 organizations that included fraternal, military, benevolent, church, drinking, temperance, workers', and sportsmen's associations, along with the E Clampus Vitus and the Pickerel and Sazarac Lying Clubs. As members of these clubs, the boys met, marched, prayed, socialized, drank, ate, politicized, formed committees, promoted their own welfare, took care of orphans and widows, and lied.

Most of the boys still liked to hunt and shoot. In town, they shot billiards and each other. Out in the wild, they shot Indians, Chinese, Mexicans, and each other. Sometimes a stray bullet missed the hare and wiped out the hound.

In the early days, any game was fair game, and there were no limits. Hunters shot quail, jays, robins, and pigeons; rabbits, squirrels, porcupines, and bobtail rats; deer and bear; wild cats and tame cats; wild boars, maundering cows, and domestic chickens; game birds, tame birds, and song birds. They stalked ladies of the night and the fabled and illusive snipe.

They didn't always bag their game. At a planned turkey shoot in Colfax, the cargo of turkeys ordered live arrived on the train dressed and ready for the oven, which resulted in a good cussin' contest but no shooting.

To the boys, the count was more important than the need. In 1881, 10 hunters killed 560 doves. Although hunters later swore that quail moved into the city during hunting season, they could still tote up a kill of 58 in a day.

Fishing was good. On a fishing trip to Lake Faucherie, leading citizens Dibble and Fletcher caught 85 fine trout in one afternoon and 52 the following morning. On a later trip to Lake Tahoe, Dibble—the State Fish Commissioner—and a fellow fisherman caught 254 fish weighing 260 pounds in 6 hours.

Lawyer Hupp swore that on his fishing trip he didn't keep count after the first 300; but on the way back, he handed so many out to his many friends he arrived home with only one.

Judge Walling had an even better story. When he shot and mortally wounded a bear in the mountains, the bear rolled down a steep hill and gained such momentum it rolled half way up another hill, then back down, and back and forth until the bear was so badly battered it

7-C Ranch
CRACKER BOX:
THE OSBORN CABIN

M. STARKEY

was unrecognizable. The only piece of proof the Judge could produce was a bit of a bush the bear had rolled over.

In 1880 the local Sportsman's Club organized to enforce hunting regulations; and in 1882, a local paper agitated to stop the slaughter of Lake Tahoe trout for chicken feed.

However, too many fish could be a problem. The trout at Truckee were so thick they rubbed the scales off each other, and the rapidly multiplying trout and catfish in the city reservoirs swam through the city water system and choked pipes and garden hoses. They even stopped the presses when an 8-inch catfish got jammed in the *The Union* water-power line.

Favorite spectator sports included foot, bicycle, horse, wheelbarrow, and hare and hound races. Sport fans enjoyed cockfights, dog fights, prizefights, walking and weight-lifting contests, wrestling matches, free-for-alls, hangings, brandings, and whippings. Although respectable members of the community denounced the barbaric Spanish bear and bull fights, so many jammed into the arena one Sunday the stand collapsed and dumped about 1,000 white spectators on their moral backsides.

The boys celebrated all the traditional holidays from New Year to Christmas and some no-longer-so-usual holidays such as Bunker Hill Day and Bastille Day and Robert Burns' and Frederick von Schiller's 100th birthdays. At the drop of an invitation they attended firemen's balls, masquerade balls, and bald-headed balls. They danced in homes and hotels, sawmills and flour mills, schoolhouses and the courthouse; and when women were scarce, they danced with each other.

They ate. At a Fourth of July barbecue, 3,000 loaves of bread, 80 pounds of ham, 8 sheep, 4 bullocks, and 4 large hogs were served to 1,500 people. When a freight train wrecked near Boca and killed 90 sheep, the Washoe Indians built a bonfire and held an even bigger barbecue.

When the roller skating mania hit in the 80s, everyone roller skated in indoor arenas—the young, the old, the single, the married, the fallen, and the reverend. This was the mania that led to Reverend Stump's fall from grace.

In winter, they ice skated, snowshoed, skied, tobogganed, and ice fished. When the ice course was in tip-top condition in Nevada City dignified judges and dandified lawyers joined the younger boys yelling "Track!" as they zipped down Broad to the Plaza.

In summer, they played cricket, baseball, and football. They wrestled, fenced, and bowled. They got into name-calling contests and pistol duels. They played euchre, whist, poker, checkers, and dominoes. They rode boats down water flumes and sighted sea serpents in Lake Tahoe.

They enjoyed dove stews. In 1884, the Sportsman's Club cooked their game into a stew in the woods while the sportsmen told nothing but the truth about their mighty exploits.

When the local hunting and fishing scenes got too crowded with club members, sportsmen hiked to Lake Tahoe to rusticate. In time, the rustication became sophisticated. As more people took to retreating, more lavish accommodations followed. Tents and blankets gave way to huts, which gave way to high-rise hotels, plush condominiums, and lush lakefront villas.

Today, the bear and bull fights have moved to Wall Street, and the glitzy gambling casinoes have retreated to Lake Tahoe. But back in the woods, real sports can still find little crackerbox cottages where they can rusticate and recreate far from the madding crowd.

Troublesome Truckee: 125 and Troublesome No More

Troublesome Truckee: 125 and Troublesome No More

TRUCKEE HAS LONG BEEN somewhat of a step-city in Nevada County, not being born until 1863, never a mining camp, and on the extreme edge of both the county line and "civilized" society. With the coming of the Central Pacific railroad through Coburn's Station in 1868 this way station through the Sierra began to bustle and bubble and get into a whole lot of trouble. After Coburn's Station went up in smoke in July 1868, the town was rebuilt and renamed Truckee.

When the first passenger train passed through, everyone celebrated and the town was painted such a bright red it took many years for the paint to wear off.

Truckee quickly and easily earned and deserved the reputation of a wild and wooly railroad and lumbering town where the liquor ran freely, gambling was nonstop, shootings, brawls, and brouhahas were frequent, most of the ladies were professionals in hurdy-gurdy houses, and the men worked like mules to earn money they spent like asses.

With the coming of the railroad, the area prospered as its natural resources and products began to be shipped throughout the country. Much of the railroad itself and the mines in the Washoe silver lode were built from Truckee timber. Primeval forests were not only reduced to logs and lumber but to boxes, shingles, charcoal, pulp, and paper and shipped out. Ice companies harvested thousands of tons of natural ice each winter and shipped it out. Some of the ice went east and some went to cool some of the hellfire-like Washoe mines. The Boca Brewing Company brewed thousands of barrels of beer each year and shipped it out—as far as Paris for the World's Fair in 1883. Sheep and dairy and beef cattle were fattened on the lush high-meadow grasses in the summer, and their fleece, butter, and carcasses were shipped out. Tons of succulent native trout were harvested from lakes and streams and shipped out. However, Truckee had one staple export that the rest of Nevada County would have liked to do without.

The bad men and fallen frails who gravitated to Truckee and got into trouble were shipped to the county jail in Nevada City. Whenever local papers toted up the prisoners, which they often did, Truckee usually scored tops. If the number of inmates got low, Truckee could always be relied upon to ship in a fresh supply.

Truckee was tolerant of just about anything or anybody—except Chinese. Truckee not only joined the general cry, "The Chinese must go!" they made sure they went. In late 1888, eight remaining Chinese were requested to leave town. Five sold their buildings and left. Then there were three. One was convicted of giving opium to Indians. He paid his fine and left. Then there were two. Soon there were none. By the late 1890s, the Chinese had been bullied and boycotted out of Truckee.

A vigilante committee, the "601," also periodically routed roughs, toughs, and other undesirables. Truckee would bask in purity for a short time, then back came the bad.

As little settlements of boarding houses and saloons sprang up around the scattered lumber, ice, and brewery centers, so did trouble.

Although some of Truckee's exuberant and raucous behavior in the early days could be blamed on youth and isolation, Truckee and its

74

THE STAR HOTEL
TRUCKEE CALIFORNIA
MARILYN STARKEY

neighbors didn't mellow with age. In 1888, Truckee was twenty-five and still troublesome.

According to a Reno paper, Truckee, the "Vag's Mecca," was still colored red. Lights flared over gambling dens and beckoned from houses of ill fame to lure men in and part them from the wages they earned by swinging their axes in the forest. What the saloon keepers and the demimondes didn't get, the blackleg gamblers did. Then, back to the forest they trod—none the wiser from their brief spree—to clear the booze from their brains and strengthen their bodies, which would weaken to the same lures come next payday.

The local paper agreed and summed it up this way. Truckee is a hell of a town where toughs, thugs, pimps, prostitutes, gamblers, tramps, idlers, vagabonds, vagrants, tin-horn gamblers, back-street dudes, opium fiends, and petty thieves thrive. With a population of about 1,500, Truckee furnishes more crime and criminals than the rest of the 20,000 citizens in the county. Why is this? Because it's a railroad town? Bosh! Reno, Winnemucca, and Elko are all nice, orderly, railroad towns. Truckee is bad because it is permitted to be bad. Crime is winked at or considered to be a sport. That's why Truckee was troublesome, and Truckee was not alone.

On a typical bad day in Boca, the German brewery workers who toiled on one side of the Truckee River and the Irish sawmill workers who toiled on the other side would meet in a local saloon and try to eliminate each other. One payday in '88, the log drivers "ginned up" and painted the town their favorite shade of red. When they couldn't find any brewery men to pound on, they pounded on each other until one was shot and killed. That sobered Boca, but only temporarily.

Then, yet another drunk was hit and killed by a train. The railroad company who owned the land decreed: no more talkin', fightin', or cryin' whiskey would be served in Boca barrooms. Too many drunks got into too many free-for-alls or passed out on the railroad tracks and got smashed by passing trains.

They wept, they wailed, they gnashed their teeth, then the Boca saloon keepers merely moved across the river and up sprang Rodsville where the liquor was potent enough to kill from a rod away.

In time, some of Truckee's rowdy neighbors disappeared, and troublesome Truckee gradually transformed into the more moral and sedate history- and tourist-conscious Truckee. By the time Truckee was 50, tourists flocked to her pure-as-the-new-fallen-snow Winter Carnivals and sporting events, and Hollywood discovered Truckee to be a winter-wonderland filming paradise.

This year, Truckee is 125 and troublesome no more. A nicer, more orderly little railroad town—with historical attractions, such as the Star Hotel and the Jail Historical Museum—you couldn't hope to find even in Elko.

Washed Down and Washed Up, But Not Out

Washed Down and Washed Up, But Not Out

At first it was San Juan, a name taken from a nearby hill named by Christian Kientz, the first miner-settler in the area in 1853. Why such a name? Historians disagree. Maybe it reminded Kientz of the hill on which stood the castle of San Juan d'Ulloa that he passed while soldiering with General Scott in Mexico. Maybe the words popped miraculously from his devout Catholic lips or, possibly, his fervent Masonic lips when he first viewed the hill. Of course, he could have just picked one of the many Spanish names on the land from San Andreas to San Rafael, or it could have been named by someone historically unhailed. But San Juan it was, and it developed like most mining camps.

As miners began to pour in, Kientz built a home and opened a hotel. Soon, two provision stores were thrown up. More houses and a National Hotel came in 1855, then more hotels and stores, followed by frequent fires, the Chinese, and some resettlers who named some streets—San Francisco, Bush, and Maiden Lane—after those they had left behind in San Francisco. When the post office was established in 1857, North was added, as San Juan was already taken. From then on the history of North San Juan gets somewhat less exciting.

After the town water system was installed in '62, the Hydraulic Hose Company was organized. The fire department didn't need a fire engine. The water pressure was so great water could be squirted to any part of town; however, in '70, a fire wiped out Chinatown.

By 1880, North San Juan with a population of about 900 people and 100 Chinese was hailed as the business, mining, and intellectual center of the many mining camps scattered on the "Ridge." Businesses were: drug, clothing, grocery, book, hardware, furniture, millinery, jewelry, dry goods, boot and shoe, and bakery and confectionery stores; blacksmith, carpenter, wagon, barber, and tin and iron shops; three saloons and three breweries; two hotels; a livery stable, lumberyard, brush factory, and hose factory; mining offices and a bank; one dentist, two lawyers, two undertakers, and four physicians.

Mining was hydraulic. The picturesque feature of the town was a spindly, long-legged overhead flume that straddled the streets and carried water across town to mines in the outlying areas where the surrounding hillsides were washed down at a rapid rate.

Intellectual and culture institutions included: a Methodist Episcopal Church, two schools with a library, a theater, the San Juan Beer Garden, the Fire Boys Saloon, fraternal lodges, a newspaper, and Oliver Perry Stidger. Judge Stidger was the Ridge's renaissance man. He did it all: an Ohio farmer who became California hotelkeeper, merchant, miner, lawyer, judge, duelist, justice of the peace, orator, editor, and theater and newspaper owner. Stidger was twice married, bullheaded and outspoken, a Republican, school trustee, property owner, officer of an irrigation company, political irritant, library promoter, agitator for a local railroad—sometimes pro, sometimes con—target of a Southern assassin who didn't like his Northern sympathies, and a rare champion of the Chinese.

The Ridge's other great claim to fame—possibly over-claimed—was the Ridge Telephone Company. The company's 60-mile line, which had 22 stations that connected French Corral to

BIGLEY'S MARKET 1853
NORTH SAN JUAN, CALIFORNIA
MARILYN STARKEY

Milton in Sierra County, was constructed in 1878 and is claimed by some to be absolutely, without a doubt, the first long-distance telephone line in the world. With its main office in North San Juan, the system was used to tell ditch tenders in far scattered areas along the meandering water ditches when to turn water on and off for specific hydraulic operations. After hydraulic mining became illegal, it served as an early warning system when government "spies" came into the area to check on illegal mining operations. The word would go out, "Shut off the water and tie down the monitors. The Feds are coming." By the time the spies got to the site, the water was off and the miners were gone. Only the soaked soil on a dry, summer day betrayed.

The robbery of the North San Juan stage in 1866 by three masked bandits, who absconded with $7,900 from the Wells, Fargo treasure chest, set the stage for the making of a hero. As soon as word of the robbery reached Nevada City, Stephen Venard joined a posse of five who rode off in hot pursuit. The group separated. As Venard crashed out of some underbrush, one of the bandits had a dead bead on him. Venard raised his Henry repeating rifle, fired, and down went a bandit—dead. The second bandit, who also had the drop on Venard, ducked behind a rock. When he peeked over the rock, Venard fired his Henry, and two were dead. As Venard jumped into some bushes, he landed in the middle of the stolen loot, which he covered with leaves, then dashed after the third bandit who crashed up a hillside. Venard aimed and fired and down fell the third who was dispatched with shot number four. The newborn hero was given one-half of the $3,000 reward and a new Henry rifle and was made a Nevada County deputy and a lieutenant colonel in the California National Guard. Venard's only regret was that he had wasted one shot.

In 1884, after much of the Nevada County landscape had been washed down and out and landed in low-land farmlands, old hydraulic techniques were outlawed. With the hydraulic mines washed up, many of the small communities on the Ridge gradually disappeared. North San Juan was down, but not out. Gradually, miners dropped their illegal hydraulic hoses and picked up spades and plows and planted gardens, orchards, and vineyards.

Although North San Juan fell somewhat behind the times, it survived. In 1915, twelve telephone subscribers were connected to the "outside world" for the first time. The long-distance business line was gone, but private lines had at long-last reached the Ridge. Then, in 1939, North San Juan stepped out of the dark ages when wires were stretched into the area and North San Juan turned on and tuned in to electric lights, radios, and appliances. No longer need people in North San Juan live and die by lamp light, although a few still do.

Little remains of the grand excitement of these former times. The religious and business center of the Ridge has shifted to the Ananda Village on the outskirts of town. Some of the gardens have been removed to remote areas where small cash crops are raised. Only a few historic buildings remain, such as Bigley's Market and the Brass Rail Tavern, which serve as the cultural center of the town where you can pick up some basic survival supplies of groceries and a brew and the latest news—if there is any.

Booming a Blooming Paradise— Chicago Park at 100

Booming a Blooming Paradise— Chicago Park at 100

As THE GOLD FIELDS BECAME overcrowded and the gold became harder to get, some rushers looked around for easier ways to make a living. A few who had been farmers before became farmers again. They gave up prospecting in sterile sands and started cultivating fertile fields, and it paid. In the fall of 1850, a gardener who plowed a piece of land near Sacramento netted $2,100 from a wagon load of onions that would have sold for about $30 in a more civilized society.

Simmon P. Storms was one of the first to establish a large ranch in what is now Chicago Park and make a profit from catering to the desires and the needs of the rushers. Simmon raised vegetables and livestock, which he sold, along with mining tools, provisions, and liquor. He boarded weary travelers and stock. He traded with the Nisenan Indians, which was profitable as at first they knew little of the value of the gold they exchanged for beads. He also cashed in on their friendship and the boys' insatiable thirst for entertainment. In July 1852 a flyer invited everyone to come and see 1,000 Indians with their war implements, squaws, and papooses celebrate their annual feasts and fancy dances at Storms' Rancho. At other times, foot races, wrestling matches, shooting contests, bull and bear fights, and dog jangling events drew large crowds to Storms' sporting arena. In 1855, Storms, as a government agent, began to lead many of the local Indians out of Nevada County for resettlement in other areas.

While some other early settlers in the Chicago Park area cultivated farms and orchards, others found different uses for the local natural resources. Where settlements popped up, trees were felled and hacked into crude building materials. Italian woodcutters converted the forest primeval into firewood or charcoal that was used as fuel in local mines. In the 1870s, Joseph Shebley corralled water on Butterfly Creek and developed attractive ponds and— probably—the first fish hatchery in California.

In 1872, the old Storms' Ranch and other nearby acreage were bought by brothers John and Edward Coleman, local mine owners and entrepreneurs who also knew how to make a buck. In 1874 with the Coleman brothers acting as directors, the Nevada County Narrow Gauge Railroad was organized. When the line that ran from Colfax by way of Grass Valley to Nevada City was completed in 1876 it ran right smack through the Colemans' property and past their sawmill, which furnished lumber for the construction and operation of the railroad. While orchardists and ranchers along the line were jumping for joy because they could now ship their produce by rail and reach distant markets more quickly and cheaply, land prices also took a jump. Although land that a few years earlier had sold for $5 an acre was selling for $100 and $200 an acre, a land investor couldn't miss "no matter where he drove his peg."

By 1886, the Nevada County Promotional Committee was booming the area as a blooming paradise. Nevada County had: fertile lands at low prices, plenty of water for irrigation, a temperate climate, plump and firm children, intelligent and cultured citizens, palatial residences and neat cottages, beautiful lawns and gardens, excellent schools, and imposing churches. Nevada County did not have: thun-

CHICAGO PARK SCHOOL
MARILYN STARKEY

derstorms or sandstorms, cyclones or tornadoes, malaria or mosquitoes, fogs or floods. Admittedly, Nevada County wasn't "exactly Paradise." The weather had a few "bad aspects," and people did grow old and die.

This type of hype soon got a bite from a group of investors in Chicago, Illinois, who bought about 6,000 acres and devised a plan to develop an elaborate townsite near Storms' Station on the rail line. Town lots priced from $75 to $100 were laid around a public square. Large tracts of 10- to 30-acre "villas" that surrounded the townsite were priced at $75 an acre. Within the townsite, large areas were reserved for two churches, an academy, a large park, and an elaborate three-story, 80-room, $30,000 Hotel Lissenden.

By late 1887, 3,000 acres had been sold and buyers from Illinois and surrounding states began to arrive. Land was cleared, fruit trees were ordered, Storms' Station became the Chicago Park Station, and the Chicago Park *Times* was published. In January 1888, the Chicago Park Colony plat was filed with the recorder. Miracle of miracles, saloons were forbidden in the townsite! Paradise was almost at hand.

Soon after, Chicago Park was blessed with a post office and a baseball team. February 1888 marked a momentous event when a small group congregated and dug a historical hole in which was planted the first tree—a cherry tree—in a Chicago Park orchard.

Then discord arose. The baseball team splintered into two groups, and a couple of "kickers" complained so loudly about the slow progress of the colony their carps were heard and repeated in Illinois papers. Satisfied settlers responded that it would be best if bags of wind who could never raise anything but dust in summer would stay away.

Wind bags and summer dust were not the worst problem in paradise. In the winter of 1889–1890, the Snow King established a reign over the area that all future snowstorms were measured by. As word of this "bad aspect" of Nevada County weather—jokingly called Chicago Park orange blossoms—drifted east, potential settlers cancelled their trip, but paradise was not lost.

Although the elaborate plans for the Chicago Park Colony fizzled, stickers stayed and others came to settle and developed productive orchards that consistently won prizes at local and state fairs and found profitable markets in San Francisco, the east, and China.

In time, culture came to Chicago Park in the forms of a church, farm bureau, garden club, and school. The first school in Chicago Park was built in 1898 from material left over from the defunct townsite project. In time, the school was enlarged and modernized and the outhouses were moved inside. There, generations of "plump and firm children" from the area began their transformation into "cultured citizens" until a new school was opened in 1966.

This year, 1988, Chicago Park became 100 years old, and she still blooms like a blushing maiden each spring. Now, like Simmon Storms before them, some of the orchardists sell their produce and wares to the trampling tourist herd that pass their wayside stands and restaurants.

Cow Tales at the End

Cow Tales at the End

STRANGE AS IT MAY SEEM, cows played an important part in the history of Nevada County. If you disregard the Indians, and many did and do, cows that wandered away from a party of emigrants in the late 1840s were the first to settle in the area for a few days while they munched up the luxurious grass in the little grassy valley that, in time, became Grass Valley.

Many gold-rush tales indicate that it was lucky for a prospector to have a cow handy not only to provide milk or fresh meat or beef jerky, but as a sort of a gold lodestone.

According to one of these early cow tales, a miner discovered pay dirt in the belly of a cow. The tale is not as farfetched as it sounds as several small nuggets were found in local chickens and even embedded in potatoes.

In 1850 while out chasing his cow, George Knight stubbed his toe and kicked up one of the first gold-quartz ledges in the area.

A Rough and Ready man in pursuit of the family cow stumbled over a nugget that assayed at over $1,200.

While watching a neighbor shoo a cow out of his garden by squirting water in its face with a hose, L. A. Pelton was struck with the idea of the Pelton wheel, which revolutionized the use of water power in hard-rock mining. At least, that's the cow tale most widely told.

In 1880, a man in Dutch Flat picked up a rock to toss at bossy and, sure enough, the rock contained $100 in gold.

Only a few years ago, in a Sierra meadow, a man kicked what he thought was a "cow pie" only to discover he had kicked up one of the largest gold nuggets found in recent history. So, when out chasing bossy, it certainly paid to watch not only where you stepped but what you picked up.

In the early days, cows and pigs bunked around or under the early miners' crude huts; but with the coming of the ladies and civilization, attempts were made to remove livestock to a more respectable distance—with more or less luck.

Cattle, which were herded right through the main streets on their way to and from winter pastures, stomped up clouds of dust that settled on newly polished furniture to the dismay of fastidious housewives. They also left calling cards wherever they pleased.

Such old varieties of cattle, which bore little resemblance to sweet-faced, no-horned, modern-day Bossy, were dangerous and not to be messed with. Local newspapers carried many reports of people being gored and seriously injured or killed.

In 1861, a ferocious bullock charged people aside on Main Street in Nevada City, tried to jump over Little Deer Creek, landed in a flume, and was whooshed into Deer Creek—dead on arrival. When another long-horn kicked up his horns and his heels on the streets of Nevada City, sure-shot Steve Venard felled him with three shots.

In time, almost everyone had a milch cow or a few head of cattle that showed little respect for property lines. As the cattle increased so did the beefs. Livestock that wandered into yards and gardens and massacred plots of pet petunias created ill-will and sometimes an ill cow. The flower people rejoiced when an overdose of an oleander did in a cow on the loose.

As battle lines were drawn, flower power eventually won an ordinance that prohibited

STAR BARN
GRASS VALLEY, CA
MARILYN STARKEY

livestock from running loose in the Grass Valley city limits. Unfortunately, cows had no more respect for ordinances than property lines.

In the summer of '68 in a letter to the editor, a cow owner complained that the ordinance was unfair to the poor working man who could ill afford to pay $2—almost a day's pay—to bail bossy or piglet out of the city pound. Enforcing the ordinance was also a burden on the taxpayers. They paid for a deputy poundmaster who had nothing to do but sit on a rock and listen for cow bells. Furthermore, the ordinance was corrupting youth. Young boys who were reportedly paid small sums for every cow they turned into the pound were not above dragging bossy into the city limit so they could collect their fees.

The cow controversy created such a furor that a local editor sent out a series of cow alerts and runners were sent to warn Grass Valley when a loose cow was spied making her way toward the city. The cow guards were doubled and ordered not to sleep while on watch. Despite their precautions, bossy infiltrated the picket line during the night and left behind cow signs of defiance.

Even the aristocratic came off their hill to enter the fray. In October 1888, a resident of Aristocracy Hill suggested that Nevada Street be renamed Cow Avenue or Bovine Boulevard as that was where graceful cud-chewers paraded, day and night, and devoured and destroyed property. After the cows congregated on a plaza atop the hill early each morning to ring their bells and bellow their greetings and made sure everyone was up and out of humor, they strolled off to crush sidewalks, break fences, pull down trees, and chew up shrubbery. The irate citizen kicked because not only his sidewalks but his morals were being tainted. All this commotion made him cuss before breakfast; and as he walked down the avenue, he not only had to shoo bossy out of the way but carefully pick his way through the liberal cowslips. The gentleman concluded that, since no town with any pretensions to decency and justice should permit cattle to roam, the Nevada City "dads" should pass an ordinance to compel owners to keep their bovines off the streets.

Although the battle raged on for years, bovines and pigs were gradually removed from city streets and gardens to outlying areas and housed in picturesque pastures and barns such as this one. Who knows what star quality cows this old barn may have quartered? As you whizz past the "star barn" off the Golden Center Freeway, give a thought to cows—some of the historical stars of yesteryear.

References

PRIMARY SOURCES:

Browne, Juanita Kennedy. *Nuggets of Nevada County History.* Nevada City: Nevada County Historical Society, 1983.

Browne, Juanita Kennedy. "One Hundred Years Ago in Nevada County," *The Union,* Grass Valley, California, 1979–1988.

Newspapers: *Grass Valley Telegraph, Grass Valley Union, North San Juan Times, Nevada Journal,* and the *Nevada Daily Transcript.*

Wells, Harry L. (ed.). *History Of Nevada County, California.* Berkeley: Howell-North Books, 1970.

SECONDARY SOURCES:

Comstock, David A. *Gold Diggers and Camp Followers, 1845–1851.* Grass Valley: Comstock Bonanza Press, 1982.

Comstock, David A. *Brides of the Gold Rush, 1851–1859.* Grass Valley: Comstock Bonanza Press, 1987.

Jones, Pat. *The Chicago Park Connection.* Chicago Park: Pat Jones, 1983.

Nevada County Historical Society Bulletins: Vol. 9 No. 3, Vol. 11 No. 1, Vol. 12 No. 4, Vol. 14 No. 1, Vol. 19 No. 2, Vol. 20 No. 1, Vol. 23 No. 2, Vol. 24 No. 3, Vol. 25 No. 1, Vol. 25 No. 2, Vol. 30 No. 3, Vol. 33 No. 1, Vol. 34 No. 2.

Walker, Franklin. *San Francisco's Literary Frontier.* New York: Alfred A. Knopf, 1939.

Index

(Numbers in *Italics* indicate sketches)

91